# E. E. Cummings Revisited

## Twayne's United States Authors Series

Joseph M. Flora

*University of North Carolina*

TUSAS 637

E. E. CUMMINGS IN THE 1920S, SELF-PORTRAIT SKETCH
*Courtesy of the Houghton Library, Harvard University*

# E. E. Cummings Revisited

Richard S. Kennedy

*Temple University*

Twayne Publishers • New York
Maxwell Macmillan Canada • Toronto
Maxwell Macmillan International • New York  Oxford  Singapore  Sydney

Twayne's United States Authors Series No. 637
E. E. Cummings Revisited
Richard S. Kennedy

Copyright © 1994 by Richard Kennedy

Poems by E. E. Cummings reprinted by permission of Liveright Publishing Corporation
Copyright © 1923, 1925, 1926, 1931, 1935, 1938, 1939, 1940, 1944, 1945, 1946, 1947, 1948, 1949, 1950, 1951, 1952, 1953, 1954, 1955, 1956, 1957, 1958, 1959, 1960, 1961, 1962 by E. E. Cummings
Copyright © 1963 by Marion Morehouse Cummings
Copyright © 1972, 1973, 1974, 1975, 1976, 1977, 1978, 1979, 1980, 1981, 1982, 1983, 1984, 1985, 1986, 1987, 1988, 1989, 1990, 1991 by the Trustees for the E. E. Cummings Trust
Previously unpublished writings by E. E. Cummings Copyright © 1994 by the E. E. Cummings Trust, George J. Firmage, agent
Reproductions of drawings and paintings by E. E. Cummings Copyright © 1994 by the E. E. Cummings Trust, George J. Firmage, agent

Twayne Publishers
Macmillan Publishing Company
866 Third Avenue
New York, New York 10022

Maxwell Macmillan Canada, Inc.
1200 Eglinton Avenue East
Suite 200
Don Mills, Ontario M3C 3N1

Library of Congress Cataloging-in-Publication Data

Kennedy, Richard S.
    E. E. Cummings revisited/Richard S. Kennedy.
        p.   cm.—(Twayne's United States authors series; TUSAS 637)
    Includes bibliographical references (p.  ) and index.
    ISBN 0-8057-3995-5 (alk. paper)
    1. Cummings, E. E. (Edward Estlin), 1894–1962—Criticism and interpretation.
I. Title.   II. Series.
PS3505.U334Z713   1994                                          93-4853
                                                                  CIP

The paper used in this publication meets the minimum requirements of American National Standard for Information Sciences—Permanence of Paper for Printed Library Materials. ANSI Z3948-1984.

10 9 8 7 6 5 4 3 2 1

Printed in the United States of America

*For Norman Friedman
and David Forrest,
Balloonbringers*

# Contents

# Publisher's Note

Published to coincide with the centennial of the American poet's birth, E. E. Cummings Revisited by Richard S. Kennedy draws on the voluminous Cummings Collection at the Harvard Library, including materials made available since the 1964 publication of E. E. Cummings by Barry A. Marks. We are pleased to offer this new critical study of E. E. Cummings and his unequaled literary achievement.

# Illustrations

# Preface

As a critical study of E. E. Cummings' work, with emphasis on his poetry, this book is, in some ways, a supplement to my earlier study *Dreams in the Mirror: A Biography of E. E. Cummings* (1980). I take additional pleasure in bringing it forth in this year of the one-hundredth anniversary of Cummings' birth. It is addressed to the general reader, especially the college student who is interested in modern poetry. It makes full use of the voluminous Cummings Collection in the Houghton Library, Harvard University, and of the Cummings papers in the Humanities Research Center, University of Texas, and the Cummings manuscripts at the University of Virginia.

When I published *Dreams in the Mirror* I noted in the bibliography that a segment of the Cummings Collection at Harvard, chiefly his private journals and the records of his dreams, had been restricted from research until 1991 by Cummings' wife, Marion Morehouse. Now that I have had full access to these materials I find that I had seen most of them before they were catalogued at the library and that only a portion of his journals had been withheld from me, namely, a selection of his notebooks from the mid-1930s up to the time of his death. (The early journals had been cataloged as "Notes" because Cummings had made typewritten copies of them that were not under restriction—as was also true of many of the later notebooks that had been catalogued as "Sketchbooks" or "Travel Diaries.") The information I have drawn from these newly opened papers in the Houghton Library is scattered here and there in the book, but I have made greatest use of it in the last two chapters.

I wish to say a few words here about the way folklore has spread an error about the capitalization of E. E. Cummings' name. The mistake took on written form when in 1964 Harry T. Moore stated in a preface to Norman Friedman's book *E. E. Cummings: The Growth of a Writer* that Cummings "had his name put legally into lower case." No one seems to know the origin of this piece of misinformation. Cummings always inscribed his name "E. E. Cummings" when he signed copies of limited editions of his books (and there were many of them) and signed his paintings "E. E. Cummings" (although he signed very few). The E. E. Cummings Society has attempted to correct this error by writing to editors of newspapers and magazines whenever they fail to capitalize his name. Almost thirty years later Norman Friedman published an article, "Not 'e.e. cummings,'" in *Spring, A Journal of the E. E. Cummings Society* (October 1992), revealing that Harry T. Moore had no other source than hearsay for his erroneous statement, and attempting to set the record straight once and for all. I hope these words here will also aid in correcting this widespread misconception. Cummings may have earned the title "mr. lower case," as Brad Leithauser has called him in the *New Yorker* (February 3, 1992), but he is in person "E. E. Cummings."

I should like to thank Cummings' daughter, Nancy T. Andrews, for her readiness to open her father's papers and unpublished manuscripts for research and publication, and to express my gratitude to George J. Firmage, agent for the E. E. Cummings Trust, for permission to publish quotations from Cummings' unpublished writings and especially for taking care that the texts of the poems are printed correctly. I am deeply grateful to Victor Schmalzer of Liveright Publishing Corporation for permission to quote from Cummings' published poems. I owe thanks to Leslie Morris, curator of manuscripts at Houghton Library, for permission to quote from the unpublished materials in the Cummings Collection and to use photographs of Cummings' drawings. Susan Halpert of the Reading Room staff at the Library has been especially helpful.

I wish to thank Elizabeth Gombosi of the Harvard Art Museums for her help in securing a photograph of the bronze bust of Cummings by Gaston Lachaise.

I thank Professor Joseph Flora of the University of North Carolina for a critical reading of the manuscript and Mark Zadrozny and Elizabeth Fowler for editorial oversight of this book. Special thanks are due to Nadia Kravchenko for her word-processing skills.

My greatest debt, as always, is to Ella Dickinson Kennedy, whose perceptiveness and wisdom are my surest guides in all the projects that I undertake.

Richard S. Kennedy

# Chronology

1894    Born October 14 in Cambridge, Massachusetts, son of Edward Cummings and Rebecca Haswell Clarke.

1907–1911    Prepares for college at Cambridge Latin School.

1911–1915    Harvard College. Receives A.B., "*magna cum laude* in Literature, especially in Greek and English."

1916    Receives A.M., Harvard. Begins painting in the Cubist style.

1917    Moves to New York City. Volunteers for Norton-Harjes Ambulance Corps on April 7. Sails to France on April 28. After five weeks in Paris, is sent to the western front on June 13. Arrested by French security police on September 23, on suspicion of espionage. Sent to Dépôt de Triage, La Ferté-Macé. Released for return to U.S. on December 19. First book publication of poems in *Eight Harvard Poets.*

1918    Six months' duty in the 73rd Infantry Division, Camp Devens, Massachusetts.

1919    Love affair with Elaine Thayer, wife of Scofield Thayer. Daughter, Nancy, born December 20.

1920    Begins a lifetime of periodical publication when his poems appear in the *Dial.*

1921    Lives in Paris until October 1924.

1922    *The Enormous Room,* an account of imprisonment at La Ferté-Macé.

1923    *Tulips and Chimneys,* first book of poems.

1924    Marries Elaine Thayer on March 19 in Cambridge, Massachusetts. They divorced on December 4 in Paris.

1925    *XLI Poems. &. Dial* Award "for distinguished service to American letters."

1926    *Is 5.*

1927    Marries Anne Barton on May 1. *Him,* a play, published.

1928  *Him* produced at Provincetown Playhouse.

1930  [No Title], a series of Dadaesque chapters.

1931  *ViVa. CIOPW,* reproductions of his art work. Travels to Russia.

1932  Separates from Anne Barton in October. Meets Marion Morehouse, who lives with him as his wife until his death.

1933  *Eimi,* account of trip to Russia. Guggenheim Fellowship. Travels to Paris and Tunesia.

1934  Divorces Anne Barton on August 31.

1935  *No Thanks.* Travels to California and Mexico. *Tom,* scenario for a ballet.

1938  *Collected Poems.*

1940  *50 Poems.*

1944  *1 x 1.*

1946  *Santa Claus,* a play.

1948  Reunion with daughter, Nancy.

1950  *Xaipe.* Harriet Monroe Prize by *Poetry* magazine. Fellowship of the Academy of American Poets.

1951  Second Guggenheim Fellowship. Travels to Paris, Venice, Florence, and Athens.

1952–1953  Delivers Charles Eliot Norton Lectures at Harvard. Publishes *i: six nonlectures.*

1954  *Collected Poems 1923–1954.*

1955  With the agency Craymore Associates, begins a seven-year career of poetry readings at colleges and universities.

1956  Travels to Spain and Italy.

1957  Chosen as Boston Arts Festival Poet.

1958  *95 Poems.* Bollingen Prize for Poetry.

1959  Ford Foundation grant (2 years). Travels to Ireland.

1960  Travels to Sicily, Italy, Greece.

1962  Dies on September 3 in Conway, New Hampshire. *73 Poems* published the following year.

## Chapter One

# Springtime at the *Dial*

In a way, it was chance. In 1919 Scofield Thayer and James Sibley Watson, two wealthy young men with a passion for the arts, bought the failing literary periodical the *Dial,* moved into its New York City headquarters at 15 West 13th Street in Greenwich Village, and began publishing, in January 1920, what soon became the leading avant-garde magazine of art and letters in the United States.[1] E. E. Cummings happened to be one of their closest friends, going back to the days at Harvard when all three participated in editing the *Harvard Monthly.* Their invitation to Cummings to contribute his work made possible his breakthrough to a national audience with the poems and line drawings that he began to publish in the early issues of the *Dial.*

In May 1920 five of his poems devoted to spring appeared, a group that displayed most of the distinctive features of his early work. All the poems were in free verse, with unusual spacing and unorthodox punctuation and capitalization, including the lowercase "i" for self-reference, which became Cummings' poetic trademark. Cummings was delighted at his luck "in having what amounts to my own printing-press in Thayer and Watson—by which I refer to the attention which such minutiae as commas and small i's . . . get at the hands of these utterly unique gentlemen."[2]

The five poems also presented an exuberant response to life, as in the first one:

into the strenuous briefness
Life:
handorgans and April
darkness,friends

i charge laughing
Into the hair-thin tints
of yellow dawn,
into the women-coloured twilight

i smilingly
glide.    I
into the big vermilion departure
swim,sayingly;

(Do you think?)the
i do,world
is probably made
of roses & hello:

(of solongs and,ashes)

(CP, 108)

In this piece, he expresses his acceptance of whatever life brings as he charges, swims, glides into experience, aware that it involves negatives: briefness, darkness, death (in a sunset metaphor, "the big vermilion departure"). The last two lines offer a compact juxtaposition of these opposites, a world of beginnings and endings. Nuances of punctuation reinforce the attitudes: an ampersand joins the "roses & hello" more closely; a comma gives only the slightest pause before facing up to "ashes." The spacing into "stanzas"—that is, the arrangement of lines into groups of four—then allows the last line to stand by itself and to accentuate finality. The jauntiness of the slangy "solongs" conveys the tone of cheerfulness in taking whatever life offers and accepting its short span and inevitable end.

Cummings liked to startle whenever he could. The parentheses around "Do you think?" do not belong there; they belong in the next line, surrounding the intruded phrase "i do." The contrast is stressed by the fact that the two phrases involve an exchange of opinions. Uniqueness was important to Cummings too. He wrote to his father that he was proud to have been the first person to use an ampersand in a poem.[3] Probably he also enjoyed displaying the ironic stance of a jolly awareness of death.

Death hovers over another of the spring poems too, one that describes an old lady who has a flower garden, but her life, "a pink hollyhock existence," becomes identified with the flowers, which must fade and pass:

but the other
day i was passing a certain
gate,        rain
fell(as it will

in spring)
ropes
of silver gliding from sunny
thunder into freshness

as if god's flowers were
pulling upon bells of
gold        i looked
up

and
thought to myself        Death
and will You with
elaborate fingers possibly touch

the pink hollyhock existence whose
pansy eyes look from morning till
night into the street
unchangingly        the always

old lady always sitting in her
gentle window like
a reminiscence
partaken

softly        at whose gate smile
always the chosen
flowers of reminding

                                                            (*CP*, 86)

The speaker is responding here to the beauties of a spring sunshower
on a flower garden when his thoughts move to the old lady with the
"pansy eyes" who is as fragile to the touch of death as are the flowers.

Cummings' handling of spacing and line length again becomes a part
of his statement as the poem gradually develops. We have first the
speaker casually passing by "a certain gate," then a spatial pause before
metaphorical descriptions of the sunshower, "ropes of silver gliding from
sunny thunder," to which is added a simile emphasizing the sunniness:
the flowers are imagined as "pulling upon bells of gold." Another spatial
pause comes before the speaker directs his vision up at the sunny sky, the
"up" being given a single line for emphasis. But this is followed by an
"and," also given a line all to itself as if to suggest the meditation that

the sunshower on the flower garden has provoked. Another spatial pause comes before the unexpected thought, "Death"—but as we move into the next line, the word Death is now understood to begin an address to a personification and seemingly asks a question about the inevitable withering of the flowers, touched by Death's "elaborate fingers."

Only now is the old lady introduced into the thought-stream: a spatial pause prepares us for the shift of understanding. The question of Death's touch is directed toward "the always/ old lady" who looks out on her flower garden, her "gentle window" helping to characterize her. If she is an "always" old lady, she is more than a particular old lady, and we have passed beyond the "certain gate" that stood at the opening of the poem in its individuality into a mythic world in which Death touches gentle old ladies whose lives have been lived through time until they have become "like/ a reminiscence."

Another spatial pause precedes the return to the flowers that are now identified once more with the old lady as they "smile always" and are blended into the reminiscence because they are "the chosen/ flowers of reminding." But the "reminding" as the last word in the poem seems to ask for an object, and the reader is left to contribute what he or she can, given the preceding elements of the poem: the flowers are reminding old ladies of past moments that they have lived through, but are also reminding the reader that flowers and gentle old ladies fade away when touched by death's elaborate fingers. Indeed, "stanza" spacing tells us that there is no fourth line at the end of the poem, leaving us with a sense of nothingness or absence, or perhaps suspended development before the results of death's touch.

We can see in the technique of these poems Cummings' special way of implementing the tenets of Imagism as laid down by Ezra Pound, whose principles Cummings had discovered five years earlier when he was in college—to use the rhythms of common speech rather than metrical regularity, to strive for compression and precision in language, to avoid worn-out poetic diction, and to use images as the means of poetic statement.[4] But in many of his lyrics Cummings goes beyond Imagism into a mythic mode that I call his Apollonian style. It is a style that is lyric in that it expresses emotion directly; it is mythic in its materials and its idealized approach to them. Cummings' poems in this style, as seen throughout his career, are concerned with the cycles of the natural world or the essential rhythms of human life. They deal with such subjects as sunrise, sunset, snowfall, springtime, the life of plants, the flow of rivers, the changes of the moon, and the eternal presence of the stars; and with

birth, childhood, idyllic love, sexual fulfillment, the serenity of age,
death, and a possible afterlife. This style almost always employs novel
images, simple diction, casual conversational phrasing and syntax, and a
visual form that moves slowly along to create its delicate impression or
modest assertion.

Another of the five spring poems is the well-known "in Just-," a work
that falls in a special category of poems that Cummings called
"Chansons Innocentes," and that expresses a child's vision of the world:

> in Just-
> spring       when the world is mud-
> luscious the little
> lame balloonman
>
> whistles       far       and wee
>
> and eddieandbill come
> running from marbles and
> piracies and it's
> spring
>
> when the world is puddle-wonderful
>
> the queer
> old balloonman whistles
> far       and       wee
> and bettyandisbel come dancing
>
> from hop-scotch and jump-rope and
>
> it's
> spring
> and
>       the
>
>               goat-footed
>
> balloonMan       whistles
> far
> and
> wee

(*CP,* 27)

"Just-/ spring" is the sort of word coinage that we associate with a child's linguistic development, and adjectives such as "mud-luscious" and "puddle-wonderful" suggest the natural conditions that children enjoy (but that adults dislike). When the toy-bringer, the balloonman, is revealed at the end to be the god Pan—or some other mythic satyr—the poem implies that the secrets of nature can only be recognized or appreciated by children. "in Just-" illustrates more fully than the first two poems the new visually directive technique that Cummings liked to play with in his handling of spacing, his selective use of capitalization, and his compression of words together to indicate crowding or speed.

The revelation in the word "goat-footed" is prepared for as a climax by the line arrangement and spacing: one word to a line with "the" indented and "goat-footed" not only continuing that movement but also being emphasized by the larger space above and below its line. The revelation is reinforced by the capital letter inserted in "balloonMan" when this word is repeated for the third time. Spatial arrangements in Cummings' poems can contribute to meaning, but sometimes they only provide the pleasure of pattern, as in the three different arrangements of the words "far and wee." Indeed, in this "Chanson Innocente" the very repetition, three times, of the coming of the balloonman is a feature of children's songs and chants.

In the fourth poem, "spring omnipotent goddess thou dost," Cummings offers a burlesque of his Apollonian style as it begins:

spring omnipotent goddess thou dost
inveigle into crossing sidewalks the
unwary june-bug and the frivolous angleworm
thou dost persuade to serenade his
lady the musical tom-cat,thou stuffest
the parks with overgrown pimply
cavaliers and gumchewing giggly
girls and not content
Spring,with this
thou hangest canary-birds in parlor windows

spring slattern of seasons you
have dirty legs and a muddy
petticoat, drowsy is your
mouth your eyes are sticky
with dreams and you have
a sloppy body
from being brought to bed of crocuses

> When you sing in your whiskey-voice
> > the grass
> rises on the head of the earth
> and all the trees are put on edge

In the opening of this poem, Cummings uses the archaic form of the second-person singular with rather strained archness and mocks the formalities of the common poetic address to spring by characterizing her as a slatternly streetwalker with "a sloppy body/ from being brought to bed of crosuses" who sings in a "whiskey-voice." Yet in spite of the burlesque of genre the attitude is both joyous and serious, as the later portion of the poem makes clear:

> spring,
> of the jostle of
> thy breasts and the slobber
> of your thighs
> i am so very
> > glad that the soul inside me Hollers
> > > > (*CP*, 89)

This same exuberant voice continues in the fifth of these spring poems, and the language is varied only slightly. This time the poem addresses earth as a Susannah in the hands of a series of Elders—philosophy, science, and religion—who are personified as dirty old men. Although the mythic elements are thrust into the realm of satire here, the reproductive rhythms of nature are celebrated all the same. And now death is depicted as a necessary part of the cycle:

> O sweet spontaneous
> earth how often have
> the
> doting
>
> > fingers of
> prurient philosophers pinched
> and
> poked
>
> thee
> ,has the naughty thumb
> of science prodded

thy

    beauty          .how
often have religions taken
thee upon their scraggy knees
squeezing and

buffeting thee that thou mightest conceive
gods
      (but
true

to the incomparable
couch of death thy
rhythmic
lover

      thou answerest


   them only with


       spring)

                  (*CP*, 58)

The variations in spacing and line length here seem more arbitrary and less significant. At times Cummings violates typographical
norms only to be different—as with the comma that begins line ten,
or the oddly placed period in line thirteen.[5] Later in his career a
young woman from a college newspaper asked Cummings his defin-
ition of poetry. "Poetry is what's different," he replied in his idiosyncratic way.[6]

The literary public that encountered Cummings' work in the *Dial* in
the 1920s was discovering something different. The January issue of the
magazine had offered them more "Chansons Innocentes": the first, "little tree," rendered a Christmas tree in terms of giving a loving home to
a foundling; the second, "why did you go," concerned a kitten that had
disappeared. Another poem about a Wild West show contained blasphe-
mous language in praise of Buffalo Bill: "Jesus/ he was a handsome man"
(Sibley Watson's mother "raised such a cry over the 'Jesus' " that he cut
short his Christmas visit home[7]); and still others were provocative and
puzzling. What were readers to make of a serenade that began "O

Distinct/ Lady of my unkempt adoration," in which the speaker con-
fessed that his song was not similar to others?

> O Distinct
> Lady of my unkempt adoration
> if i have made
> a fragile certain
>
> song under the window of your soul
> it is not like any songs
> (the singers the others
> they have been faithful
>
> to many things and which
> die
> i have been sometimes true
> to Nothing and which lives
>
> they were fond of the handsome
> moon      never spoke ill of the
> pretty stars      and to
> the serene the complicated
>
> and the obvious
> they were faithful
> and which i despise,
> frankly . . .
>
> (*CP,* 52)

What did the readers think of a seeming parody of one of
Wordsworth's "Lucy" poems that spoke of a dead beloved in this manner?

> When all's done and said,and
> under the grass
> lies her head
> by oaks and roses
> deliberated
>
> (*CP,* 11)

The literary public was just becoming acquainted with a modern poet
who chose to run counter to all the accepted norms of poetry, one who
tried to reduce the importance of motif or theme by creating linguistic

distortions or unremarkable situations in order to focus attention on language itself or on visual presentations of language. Cummings actually felt that he was moving so far away from the conventions of poetry that he would sometimes speak of a *fait* (something made) instead of a poem and refer to an artist as a *faiteur.* Poets were people who just "made things" with language (as a student of classics he knew that to the Greeks a ποιητησ was a "maker").

The public was also getting a glimpse of a persona that Cummings was just beginning to create for himself, one associated with the lower-case "i". Over the years he developed this characterization so that it gathered hovering meanings: the underling, the downtrodden one, the humble lover, the child-in-the-man, but it was often, too, the rebel who was ready to turn language upside down for beautiful effects or, sometimes, just to explore its possibilities in visual-linguistic presentations. "The day of the spoken lyric is past," he jotted in his notes. "The poem which has at last taken its place does not sing itself; it builds itself, three dimensionally, gradually, subtly, in the consciousness of the experiencer."[8]

When Ralph Waldo Emerson read through Walt Whitman's first printing of *Leaves of Grass* in 1855, he wrote to him: "I greet you at the beginning of a great career, which yet must have had a long foreground somewhere, for such a start."[9] A perceptive critic might have greeted Cummings' poems in the *Dial* in 1920 the same way. And there had been a long foreground.

## Chapter Two

# The Development
# of a Poet-Painter:
# Cambridge, Joy Farm, Harvard

Edward Estlin Cummings was born October 14, 1894, in an imposing colonial-style family home in Cambridge, Massachusetts, a few blocks from Harvard College, where his father, Edward Cummings, was an assistant professor of sociology. The mellow atmosphere of Cambridge, the home of Henry Wadsworth Longfellow and James Russell Lowell, hung pleasantly around the childhood of Estlin Cummings, as the boy was called, and the spirit of Harvard pervaded his growing-up years, even though his father soon left his faculty post to become the Unitarian minister of the South Congregational Church in Boston.

His mother, Rebecca Haswell Clarke, from nearby Roxbury was descended from old New England stock. There were literary associations in her background, including her great-great-great aunt Susanna Haswell (whose married name was Rowson), the author of the first American novel, *Charlotte Temple*. Rebecca Cummings closely oversaw her son's literary development. She taught him to read and write, encouraged him to keep a diary beginning at age five, and read stories and poems to him every day. The Cummings family later developed the custom of reading aloud every evening so that during Estlin's grammar school years, especially in the long summer evenings spent at Joy Farm, their summer retreat at Silver Lake, New Hampshire, the family listened to chapters from Walter Scott's *Quentin Durward, Kenilworth,* and *The Talisman,* Dickens' *David Copperfield* and *The Old Curiosity Shop,* Cooper's Leatherstocking Tales, Howard Pyle's *King Arthur and His Knights* and *Robin Hood,* Jules Verne's *Twenty Thousand Leagues Under the Sea,* and other young people's classics.

Rebecca Cummings loved poetry and kept a commonplace book of favorite verses. She hoped that her son would become another Longfellow, the poet whose poems were highly revered in Cambridge and memorized by pupils in the Cambridge schools. By the time of his

11

1. THE CUMMINGS HOME AT 104 IRVING STREET, CAMBRIDGE,
MASSACHUSETTS
*Photograph by Richard S. Kennedy*

high school years at the Cambridge Latin School, Estlin was publishing
poems in the school literary magazine and sending off verses (which were
not accepted) to *St. Nicholas* and *Outdoor Life* magazine. After his uncle
George Clarke gave him a copy of Thomas Hood's *The Rhymster, or the
Rules of Rime* for Christmas, Estlin began to play with triolets, rondeaus,
ballades, sonnets, and other intricate stanza forms. He turned out poems
for all occasions: Valentine's Day, birthdays, national holidays, Mother's
Day, Christmas, and even elegies for the death of elderly relatives.
Although he accumulated a huge amount of juvenilia not worth keeping,[1] he sometimes produced lines that are surprising in their maturity of
thought and expression. For example, this first stanza of a nocturne
shows the pleasure he took in sound patterns:

> A chilly,murky night;
> The street lamps flicker low,
> A hail-like,whispering rain
> Beats 'gainst the streaked,bleak pane;
> The sickly,ghostly glow
> Of the blurred,blinking,wavering,flickering light
> Shines on the muddy streets in sombre gleams
> Like a wierd lamp post on a road of dreams.

(ETC, 170)

The following response to a visit to a crematorium with his father, "Death's Chimneys," reveals a brooding awareness of mortality, followed by a surprise in the optimistic symbol of a butterfly:

> Within,a coldly echoing floor:a terror
> Of narrow,naked walls,whitened and ghastly,
> Through whose grim hollowness,faint and incessant,
> Is heard a murmuring horror of fires communing.
> What flesh and blood,what hands and face,what beauty
> Shrivels beneath the touch of flames caressing—
> Becomes obliterate in this awful furnace?
> What life dwelt in this formless heap of ashes
> Drawn forth,—the fires subdued,the furnace opened,—
> To inhabit yon dead vault of icy marble,
> Under the day,dwelling in its own darkness,
> Under the world,shrouded in its own silence?
> What eye shall read this shadowy inscription?
> What hand upon this cold thing lay its cypress?
> What lip shall touch the silent vase of ashes?
> The body,the human body divine,burning.
>
> Without,warm flood of universal sunshine;
> And a white butterfly,hovering,soaring,ascending . . .
>
> (*ETC*, 182)

But the literary surroundings of his early years were not the only important feature of Estlin Cummings' development. The benevolent environment of home and community contributed enormously to providing an ideal childhood and youth. In the quiet leafy neighborhood near Harvard young Cummings played daily with other faculty children in games of hide-and-seek, prisoner's base, hare and hounds, blindman's buff, follow the leader, cops and robbers, and scrub baseball. In the fall the neighbor children climbed into Estlin's tree house and popped corn on its little stove; in winter they built snow forts and fought snowball battles; in spring they marched in ceremony to crown a May queen and organized a parade for Memorial Day. They produced shows with Estlin's little sister Elizabeth's dolls and his dog Rex and tried to imitate circus acts that they had seen at Forepaugh and Sells Circus, Ringling Brothers, or Bostock's Animal Show.

In the summer months Joy Farm was a boy's paradise for Estlin. The family had a small pond for swimming, a stock of animals including hens, cows, a horse, a goat that could pull a cart, a donkey that Estlin

could ride, a barn with a hayloft for hiding games and hay fights, and a
lot of nearby boulders for sliding off or hiding behind when playing
Indian. Edward Cummings taught his two children how to find their
way through the woods with compass and woodcraft. They came to
know the ways of deer, woodchucks, porcupines, rabbits, caterpillars,
and butterflies. They learned to identify birds, wildflowers, and stars.
The happiness of these early years is frequently captured in poems reflec-
tive of childhood that appear intermittently throughout Cummings'
career down to the year of his death at age sixty-seven.

At Joy Farm, Estlin tried to write a poem every day, most of them
focussing on the natural scene. Some that survive are very worthy of a
high-school boy: a representative sample are included in *Etcetera, The
Unpublished Poems of E. E. Cummings* (1983), a posthumous volume.[2]

Joy Farm touched more than Cummings' early life. After his father's
death in the 1926, his mother deeded the farm to Estlin in 1929. He
spent every summer of his life thereafter in this serene setting. His many
poems about the beauties of nature up to the time of his death had their
stimulus from his early acquaintance with country life and the yearly fill-
ing of his spiritual reservoir at Joy Farm.

## II

When Estlin entered Harvard in September 1911 he was two years
younger than his classmates, although he came well-prepared from the
Cambridge Latin School in Latin, Greek, and French, and he had read a
wide shelf of standard works in English and American literature. He
stayed for five years, taking an A.B. in 1915 and an A.M. in 1916. He
concentrated in classics and was graduated "*magna cum laude* in
Literature, especially in Greek and English." Although he responded
intensely to his study of the Greek tragedians, his work in Latin brought
him such an appreciation of the Odes of Horace that he worked out
some excellent verse translations,[3] for example, his rendering of Ode IV
from Book I, which begins

> The fetters of winter are shattered,shattered,
> And the limbs of the earth are free,—
> Spring,and the breeze that loveth the lea!
> And the old keels—gaping and tempest battered—
> Men roll them down to the sea.

(ETC, 185)

Or his handling of Ode VII from Book IV, which begins this way:

> Farewell,runaway snows! For the meadow is green,and the tree stands
> Clad in her beautiful hair.
> New life leavens the land! The river,once where the lea stands,
> Hideth and huggeth his lair.
> Beauty with shining limbs 'mid the Graces comes forth,and in glee stands,
> Ringed with the rhythmical fair.
>
> (*ETC*, 184)

These Horatian Odes appealed to young Cummings not only because he liked to write lyrics about spring but also because at an early age he could respond to that Horatian awareness of the natural cycle bringing death to human beings too.

> Hope not,mortal,to live forever,the year whispers lowly.
> Hope not,time murmurs,and flies.
> Soft is the frozen sod to the Zephyr's sandal,as wholly
> Summer drives Spring from the skies,—
> Dying when earth receives the fruits of Autumn,till slowly
> Forth Winter creeps,and she dies.
>
> (*ETC*, 184)

Translation is first-rate training for a young poet. The subject matter is supplied to him, and he can then concentrate on technique and at the same time discipline himself by holding to his model. Cummings was taking a path that other poets had followed as they developed, poets as diverse as Alexander Pope, Thomas Gray, Dante Gabriel Rossetti, and Ezra Pound.

Beyond his work in classics, Cummings ranged widely in his study of many cultures, taking courses from some of the greatest scholars of the time. He studied Dante under Charles Grandgent, German literature under Kuno Franke, Russian literature under Leo Wiener, "The Art and Culture of Spain" under Chandler Post, the chivalric literature of Europe under William Henry Schofield, Chaucer under William Nielson, and Shakespeare under George Lyman Kittredge. By the end of his five years he was one of the best-educated American literary figures of his time, T. S. Eliot, Archibald MacLeish, and Ezra Pound being his only rivals.

But Harvard developed Cummings as a poet too, especially during his year-long course in "English Versification." His professor, Dean LeBaron Briggs, required students to imitate all the poetic styles from the Anglo-

Saxon alliterative verse down to the metrical freedoms of the twentieth century and gave them exercises in all the varieties of meter and stanza form. Some of Cummings' fellow students were men he had come to know through his association with the *Harvard Monthly,* the lively literary rival to the *Harvard Advocate.* These men, his fellow editors of the *Monthly,* provided him with an introduction to modern literature. Sibley Watson introduced him to French Symbolist poetry—to Verlaine and Rimbaud—and acquainted him further with the prose-poems of Mallarmé. Scofield Thayer, three years ahead of Cummings and a return graduate student after two years at Magdelene College, Oxford, brought the work of Eliot and Joyce to Cummings' attention and widened his knowledge of the modern painters. But it was S. Foster Damon, chiefly, who became Cummings' special guide to the modern movement in the arts. He introduced Cummings to the music of Debussy, Stravinsky, and the charming musical satirist Erik Satie. He broadened Cummings' knowledge of the French Impressionists and brought him to know the work of Cézanne and *Les Fauves.* Damon took him to the Armory Show when it came to Boston, where Cummings saw his first examples of Postimpressionism and Cubism. He showed Cummings his copies of *Poetry* magazine and of Pound's anthology *Des Imagistes,* and thus exposed him to the influence of Imagism. Damon had corresponded with Amy Lowell, knew the work of Sandburg, Masters, and Lindsay, and owned a copy of Gertrude Stein's *Tender Buttons.*

This bewilderment of tendencies in the modern movement excited Cummings and pushed him toward writing poems in styles more daring and creative than those that marked his early years at Harvard, when he was publishing poems in the *Harvard Monthly* and the *Harvard Advocate* that had the lyric lushness of Keats, Rossetti, and the English decadents of the 1890s. It took a long time for this breath of innovation and iconoclasm to turn up in his poetry, partly because of the generally conservative tone of the Harvard classrooms. Cummings first displayed his full allegiance to the modern movement in an essay written for Dean Briggs and later delivered at the commencement program in 1915 as a dissertation on "The New Art." Cummings stunned the audience at the graduation exercises by discussing the sculpture of Brancusi and the Cubist masterwork of Duchamp-Villon, *Nude Descending a Staircase.* He next touched on the music of Satie, Stravinsky, Schönberg, and Scriabin. But it was his reading of some startling lines from Amy Lowell's *Sword Blades and Poppy Seeds* and his quoting from Stein's *Tender Buttons* that brought

2. E. E. CUMMINGS.
GRADUATION PHOTO FROM
THE CAMBRIDGE LATIN
SCHOOL, 1911
*Courtesy of the Houghton Library,
Harvard University*

3. E. E. CUMMINGS.
GRADUATION PHOTO FROM
HARVARD COLLEGE, 1915
*Courtesy of the Houghton Library,
Harvard University*

TWO CUBIST WORKS
BY E. E. CUMMINGS
4. *DANCERS,* OIL PAINTING 1918
*Courtesy of the SUNY College at Brockport Foundation*
5. *CHRIST,* INK SKETCH, 1915
*Courtesy of the Houghton Library, Harvard University*

laughter and puzzlement to the audience of alumni and parents who were attending. Cummings was learning to enjoy his ability to shock.

This interest in the modern arts gave impetus to another of Cummings' talents. Ever since he was a child he had exhibited skill in drawing and sketching. During his time at Harvard, he decided to extend his creative zeal into the visual arts and to try his hand at painting. His classmate John Dos Passos had a similar dual ability with language and art. He and Cummings, together with their friend Edward Nagel, the son of the French-American sculptor Gaston Lachaise, all worked in consultation and practiced to become self-taught painters during this time of new excitement and breakthrough in all fields of art.

Estlin lived at home during his early college years, but when he was a senior he moved into a residence hall within the Harvard Yard and found a good deal more freedom than he had experienced growing up in the household of a Protestant minister. His college friends introduced him to a livelier social life of drinking and girl-chasing, and the repressions of the Boston-Cambridge ethic began to lift. Conflicts with his father developed during this period too, and Edward Cummings' good intentions in guiding the life of his son and his kindly interference with his activities provoked a growing rebellion. These stirrings of Estlin's personal independence accompanied his creative experiments in verse and his increasing fascination with the modern movement in the arts.

## III

At the end of their college years in 1916, a group of eight students from Dean Brigg's poetry class, including Cummings, Dos Passos, and their conservative friend Robert Hillyer (who was to become a Pulitzer Prize winner in 1933), banded together to publish a book, *Eight Harvard Poets*. The table of contents presented the poets in alphabetical order. The first was "E. Estlin Cummings," with eight poems.

In this debut to book publication Cummings grouped four sonnets, three of them conventional in treatment. The fourth, still phrased in the "thees" and "thous" of the sonnet tradition, was a sentimental address to a chorus girl. It was a hint of things to come: time-honored poetic form jarred by banal or ugly subject matter. The other four poems were in free verse, making use of unusual spacing and unorthodox capitalization. Cummings later explained how he came to these new developments in poetic presentation on the page. He said that a door to something new had swung open for him when Foster Damon had shown him Ezra

Pound's free-verse poem "The Return." Pound's placing a word alone in a line or beginning a line partway across the page does not seem startling to us now. But at that time it was sufficiently unusual to have awakened a visual response in Cummings. He reported that Pound's treatment of a classical subject in an oblique and allusive way moved him, but that the arrangement on the page, "the inaudible poem—the visual poem, the poem not for ears but eye—moved me more."[4]

One of Cummings' poems, "The Lover Speaks," is in the mode toward which Cummings had been moving in 1916. A contemporary voice speaks in colloquial phrasing. The figures of speech are lively and unusual; it seems likely that Cummings had encountered the ideas of T. E. Hulme, the theoretician of Imagism, that were becoming known at this time: that imagery should have two qualities, "concreteness, for freshness, and novelty, especially in surprising or unusual juxtapositions of images."[5]

> Your little voice
>                 Over the wires came leaping
> and I felt suddenly
> dizzy
>                 With the jostling and shouting of merry flowers
> wee skipping high-heeled flames
> courtesied before my eyes
>                                 or twinkling over to my side
> Looked up
> with impertinently exquisite faces
> floating hands were laid upon me
> I was whirled and tossed into delicious dancing
> up
> Up
> with the pale important
>                                 stars and the Humorous
>                                                 moon
> dear girl
> How I was crazy how I cried when I heard
>                                 over    time
> and tide and death
> leaping
> Sweetly
>                 your voice[6]

CREPUSCULE

I will wade out
                till my thighs are steeped in burning flowers
i will take the sun in my mouth
and leap into the ripe air
                        Alive
                            with closed eyes
to dash against darkness
                        in the sleeping curves of my body
shall enter fingers of smooth mastery
with chasteness of sea-girls
                            will I complete the mystery of my flesh
i will rise
            After a thousand years
lipping
flowers
        And set my teeth in the silver of the moon

            THE LOVER SPEAKS

your little voice
                Over the wire czme leaping
                                    and i felt suddenly
dizzy
        With the jostling and shouting of merry flowers
wee skipping high-heeled flames
courtesied before my eyes
                        or twinkling over to my side
Looked up
with impertinently exquisite faces
floating hands were laid upon me
i was whirled and tossed into delicious dancing
up
up
with the pale important
                        stars and the humorous
                                    moon
                                        dear girl
How I was crazy how i cried when i heard
                            over time and time and death
                                                        leaping
Sweetly
        your voice

                        EPITAPH
tumbling-hair
            picker of buttercups
                            Violets
                                dandelions
And the big bullying daisies
                            through the field wonderful
Another comes
with eyes a little sorry
                        also picking flowers

6. EARLIEST INSTANCE OF CUMMINGS' LOWERCASE "I," IN "CREPUSCULE,"
TYPESCRIPT FOR *EIGHT HARVARD POETS*, 1916
*Courtesy of the Houghton Library, Harvard University*

Although the poem shifts in tone and becomes overstated in the last lines, the expressiveness of the early portion makes it the freshest poem in the book. The excitement of the speaker is rushed into metaphors of flowers and flames, but each one has a further metaphorical dimension when adjectives are added. The "jostling," "shouting," and "merry" multiply the excitement and make it joyous. But "skipping" and "high-heeled" are even more apt visually for the appearance of the flames, and the metaphorical agitation becomes merged with the voice of the speaker when the "high-heeled flames" are said to have "courtesied before my eyes." These descriptions also give that jolt that Hulme was calling for. Additional metaphorical euphoria is introduced with the "impertinently exquisite faces" of the flower-flames and the "floating hands" that toss the speaker's spirit sky-high. The "Humorous" moon ends the series of metaphors, giving a jovial and understanding overlook to the whole situation of the telephone call.

In another poem, "Crepuscule," we might have had the first instance of the "small i" that later became identified with Cummings' poetic voice, but the printer, thinking it was a typographical error, twice changed it to a capital. (See illustration 6.)

The most important poem in the free-verse group is a little Imagistic masterpiece entitled "Epitaph."[7] The poem presents, obliquely, the moment before the crisis in the story of Hades' abduction of Persephone to the underworld.

> Tumbling-hair
>          picker of buttercups
>                   violets
> dandelions
> And the big bullying daisies
>                 through the field wonderful
> with eyes a little sorry
> Another comes
>         also picking flowers

The lack of punctuation in the poem allows for a double reading of one of the phrases: the daisies are "through the field wonderful," but "wonderful" can also modify another noun: "through the field wonderful . . . / Another comes." The capital "A" on "Another" begins to give mythic significance to the scene in the same way that myth entered the poem about the "balloonMan." The final phrase, "also picking flowers," refers us back to the beginning, and we realize as the poem comes to a close, that she is the flower that he will pick.

7. PRIVATE E. E. CUMMINGS, 1918
*Courtesy of the Houghton Library, Harvard University*

It is worthwhile to observe that in his first book publication there is range and diversity in the poems Cummings chose to include. The compactness of "Epitaph" seems a world away from the wordiness of the four sonnets, and the liveliness of "The Lover Speaks" is at odds with the soberness of most of his other poems included in the collection.

## IV

*Eight Harvard Poets* was due to be published in late 1917, but international events caught up with all these young men. By May 1917 four of them, including Cummings, had enrolled in the Norton-Harjes Ambulance Corps attached to the French army. Cummings had volunteered the day after the United States entered the war against Germany. His adventures were to be many, all set down in *The Enormous Room,* which will be discussed in Chapter 4. They involved a few months of duty in France, followed by a period of four months in a French concentration camp. When he was released he was drafted into the United States Army and spent seven months at Camp Devens in Massachusetts before the war was over and he was discharged.

At this point Cummings' career took a turn. Although he was still writing poems, he now began to spend the bulk of his time and creative energy trying to become a Cubist painter. For the rest of his life he continued to paint with a seriousness of purpose that never seemed to flag, although his painting style changed from Cubism to variations of modern techniques and finally to realistic representations of still life, landscape, and portrait. Yet he never had success in this side of his dual career. It served mostly to stimulate his literary talent and provide him with another perspective for the way he looked at language.

## Chapter Three

# How to Become Unique
# While Following the Trends

In developing his personal styles E. E. Cummings had two intensely creative periods in his early career. The first occurred during the six months, June through December 1916, after graduation from Harvard with his A.M. degree. He had by now accumulated a substantial hoard of poems, which he listed in what he called "Index 1916."[1] These consisted of a good many traditional poems that had appeared in the college literary magazines plus double as many, written mostly during his last college year, arranged in groups according to metrical or stanza form: sonnets, ballades, villanelles, blank verse, Sapphics, and so on. In addition, one large group of fifty-nine poems, labelled simply "D.S.N." (Designato Sine Nomine?), gathered together all his unrhymed poems without regular meter, that is, those in free verse: long-lined Whitmanesque poems, short-lined poems like French vers libre, and short Japanese forms like the haiku. These were the most personal and innovative poems in the whole assembly. Many of them were later published in somewhat different versions in his first book of poems, *Tulips and Chimneys* (1923); for example, one on the list, "In just-Spring," was an early version of "in Just-" without spatial guidance and the manipulation of lowercase and capital letters.

Cummings worked every day, playing with his typewriter, revising much of what he had on hand, making some poems more compact, scattering others on the page for visual effect, reducing his capitals to lowercase, including the personal pronoun "i", in most of the others. The effect of his interest in Cubism is apparent in one poem describing the sunset in a city, but employing imagery in which city rectangularity bumps against the traditional presentation of the dissolving colors of sunset. It is also the first instance in which he tried using verbs as nouns. As the poem develops it offers a cityscape changing at twilight from the noise of the day to the quiet at night. In the first part of the poem the unusual diction gives a sense of wrenching and stress, and the

harsh consonant sounds—*g,p,k,z*—in clusters ("rasp," "gaze") suggest
noise and clash:

> writhe and
> gape of tortured
>
> perspective
> rasp and graze of splintered
>
> normality
>                         crackle and
>                         sag
>     of planes        clamors of
>     collision
>     collapse        As
>
> peacefully,
> lifted
> into the awful beauty
>                         of sunset
>
>                         the young city
> putting off dimension with a blush
> enters
> the becoming garden of her agony
>
>                                    (*CP*, 61)

   The alliterative sounds intensify the meanings of the words and also
draw them together so that the "collapse" is more "crackly" and the
"collision" is more "clamorous." Suddenly the "l" sounds in "peaceful-
ly," "lifted," and "awful" bring a change of tone as sunset colors soften
the harsh perspective. The personified city disrobing herself of angu-
larity in pinkish dusk becomes more natural, and thus associated with
a garden.
   Since Cummings' use of lowercase typography, and especially the
small "i" for self-reference, later became the personal logography that
marked his poems, it is worthwhile to linger over an account of how
he happened to adopt this particular practice. It seems that when he
decided to choose some method of appearing unique among his contemporaries he imitated the practice of the ancient Greeks who did
not use capital letters at the beginnings of sentences nor at the beginnings of lines of poetry (except for the first letter in a poem). As for

```
In just-Spring                          ————
When the world is mud-luscious          ————        .
The queer old baloon-man                ————
Whistles far and wee,                               ————
And Bill and Eddy come pranking         Okay

From marbles and from piracies,
And it's Springtime.

When the world is puddle-wonderful      ————
The little lame baloon-man whistles   ——
Far and wee,
And Betty and Is'bel come dancing

From hop-scotch and still-pond and jump-rope,
For it's Springtime,
And the world is ooze-suave,

And the goat-footed baloon-man
Whistles
Far      —
And
Wee.
```

8. FIRST VERSION OF "IN JUST-," WRITTEN IN DEAN BRIGGS'S COURSE,
ENGLISH VERSIFICATION, SPRING 1916. NOTE THE MARKS ON THE
RIGHT AS CUMMINGS PLANS TO REVISE THE SPACING.
*Courtesy of the Houghton Library, Harvard University*

the small "i," he was intrigued and charmed by the semiliterate letters
of a New Hampshire handyman, Sam Ward, who looked after Joy
Farm when the Cummings family was away, and so Cummings decided to use the "i" as his special poetic signature. Here is an excerpt
from one of Sam's letters, which displays his own small "i," his sudden
use of capitals, and his lack of punctuation: "i Wish to thank you for
the Check for the sept Bill for grocries of 15 dollars Everything is fine
at the farm macki and i spent a lot of time up thore to see if we could
find out whoe it was doing the toring down signs and gates now the
Hunting is over thore Wont be so much going on We have kep the
gates and signs up all right."[2]

The lowercase "i" suited Cummings very well for the personality he
wished to display: in the first place, since he wanted to be unique, the "i"
set him off from all his fellow poets, but beyond that, it was appropriate
for his temperament. He had always been smaller than his six-foot two-
inch, broad-shouldered father (he himself was only five feet eight inches
in height and frail in bodily structure) and shorter than his schoolfellows
and college classmates. Thus he felt himself to be an underling physical-
ly, and he identified with the underdog in literature, life, and international conflicts. He referred to himself in letters and journals as "our
nonhero" or "unhero," as a "small-eye poet" and as "little Estlin." But
the pose of humility masked a self-assertiveness and a readiness to reject
or rebel against whatever did not suit his taste or merit his approval.
This stance of individualism had been nurtured by his New England
upbringing and by the teachings of his father. "How I hated my father
for making me read Emerson's 'Self-Reliance,' " he said in later years,
"but now it is my Bible."[3]

During the later months of 1916 Cummings was experimenting with
many different visual arrangements on the page and often tried out
slang or street language. He wanted to avoid standard poetic diction in
his work. He drew up lists of jokes and phrases from comic strips, vaudeville acts, and burlesque-house comedians and set down scraps of talk
overheard on the Boston streets. He was searching for truly colloquial
expression, which he would then arrange in poetic patterns so that the
formality of the literary presentation would clash with the grubbiness of
the material or the banality of the language. For instance, in one visual
scheme that he worked out he lined up the words in columns across the
page according to vowel sounds. The subject was a conversation with a
drunken woman about two buttons snipped off her coat:

```
        two        brass     buttons off
        your       scar let              coatlo
                       ret taone         old  dint
                       ed                             and
    a   new                 one
        you                          don't              re
                    mem
              ber
        you  were       drunk
                   when
i                   askedret ta    for                        the
                                     rose  in
              her                                                    hair
        you       can't                          havethatshe
    smiled                                        lar     riehe
                                          give           methe
              bloom
        aint                             itpretty
                       but               kid
        you            gut
    a
knife                      yes          op'  nit    thanks
my                                                          teeth
    aint                       strong   it's           the
        booze       gets 'm                     and    she
                                                hands  methe
        two        brass     buttons
                   nev
          er                                    drink
dear
```

Cummings' notes indicate that he was speculating about the relationship between the visual appearance of the words on the page and the
sounds of syllables as they would be placed on a sound-frequency scale:
"Note: in music there are (12) units which differ in pitch, corresponding
to the (19) vowel sounds. BUT the representation of the occurrence of
any and all these units by a common symbol, whose form (or picture)
changes only to portray prolongation, confers a suitability to horizontal
progression, which does not exist in the case of a fait where the sounds
(units) are presented by visible equivalents . . . calling for vertical progression."[4] He then tried this dialogue in a horizontal progression as if
his syllables were musical notes on a staff.

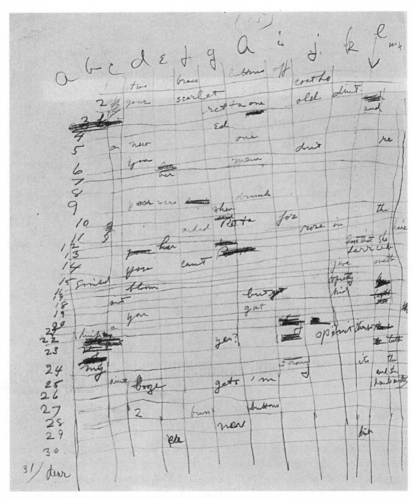

9. MANUSCRIPT OF "TWO BRASS BUTTONS," 1916
*Courtesy of the Houghton Library, Harvard University*

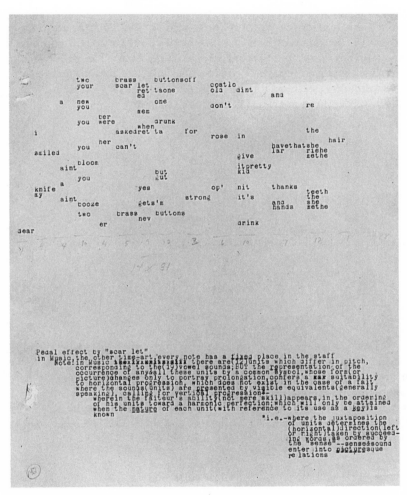

**10. TYPESCRIPT OF "TWO BRASS BUTTONS" WITH COMMENTARY, 1916**
*Courtesy of the Houghton Library, Harvard University*

During this same period he was examining other effects of sound too. He laid out schemes of vowel sounds, such as *br, bl, dr, dzh,* and so on. He would then draw up lists of words with vowel-consonant combinations, such as *breast, bless, blabbed, rabble, riddle, ladder.* He would finally select such words in sequences to form lines of verse. Sometimes the subjects were ugly ones and for these a predominance of glottal and labial sounds was appropriate. Here is one such scheme:

> of bunged mug
> blousy gob
> glued lipped
> muddle lidded
>
> ole liz
> goggle glimmed
> bag bodied
> pimple bummed
>
> slow slob-
> bers down
> babble belly
> blubber boobied[5]

Reams of paper from this period testify to Cummings' earnest exploration of the possibilities of language according to sound, typographical arrangement of space and line, grammatical twisting, unorthodox punctuation, peculiar juxtaposition of noun and adjective, or fragmentation of words and sentences. At the same time, he set down theoretical notes about poetry, music, painting, sculpture, and dance and their interaction or merging, which could create new effects in art.[6]

## II

During the months of this kind of tinkering with language Cummings was working out the features of a personal style—or styles. All this effort continued to roil in his head while he was in France, first in Paris, later on the western front with the Norton-Harjes Ambulance Corps and then in the French concentration camp at La Ferté-Macé, although he did not have much time alone to write poems. His next highly creative period occurred, surprisingly enough, during the seven months he spent in infantry training at Camp Devens, from July 1918 to January 1919. He had time to himself in the evenings or on Sundays at the Camp Devens library or the YMCA recreation hall, reading (he had just encountered Joyce's *Ulysses,* which was running in installments in the *Little Review*), writing poems, and jotting down theoretical notes on the arts.

He turned out sonnets by the dozen, for in spite of his explorations of new forms, his lyric impulse was still vigorous. Matured by practice and stimulated by a mixture of feelings—yearning for love, loneliness, nostalgia for premilitary scenes, introspective searches—his Apollonian style developed fully, as such poems as this testify:

> a wind has blown the rain away and blown
> the sky away and all the leaves away,
> and the trees stand.   I think i too have known
> autumn too long
>
>                              (and what have you to say,
> wind wind wind—did you love somebody
> and have you the petal of somewhere in your heart
> pinched from dumb summer?
>                                O crazy daddy
> of death dance cruelly for us and start
>
> the last leaf whirling in the final brain
> of air!)Let us as we have seen see
> doom's integration.........a wind has blown the rain
>
> away and the leaves and the sky and the
> trees stand:
>                the trees stand.   The trees,
> suddenly wait against the moon's face.
>
>                                              (*CP,* 153)

But by 1918 he had behind him an accumulation of experience that altered both the matter and manner of much of his work. He had left Cambridge and the repressions of life as a minister's son; he had discovered the zest of living in New York; he had sojourned in Paris with all its sexual freedom; he had endured the brutalities of La Ferté-Macé; he had absorbed the realities of army life at Camp Devens. His sensibilities had been both titillated and bruised, and his observation of human life had shown him an extensive variety of human behavior.

The impact of these excitement-filled years showed up in two kinds of poems. The first reflected Cummings' move in the direction of the new

realism and naturalism in the American arts. American painting had
seen the ascendancy of the group of realistic painters known as "the
Eight," with such leaders as Robert Henri and his portraits of immigrants, John Sloan and his pictures of elevated railways and raucous bar-
rooms, and their follower George Bellows and his famous paintings of
prize fighters. The naturalism in the fiction of Theodore Dreiser, Frank
Norris, and Sherwood Anderson had been reflected in the poetry of Carl
Sandburg, Edgar Lee Masters, and Vachel Lindsay. In this spirit
Cummings began to write sonnets and free-verse vignettes that presented nightclubs, crowded tenement districts, ethnic restaurants, prostitutes and their customers, bums, drunks, and gangsters. These subjects,
especially those dealing with sex, had long been considered "unpoetic" in
New England and unsuitable for the matter of verse. In taking up this
material Cummings played with that most revered poetic form, the sonnet. For instance, the poem below is a perfectly regular Petrarchan sonnet that, like Shakespeare's praise of the "dark lady," runs counter to the
conventional celebration of the beloved's fair hair, cherry-kissed lips, and
teeth of pearl:

> my girl's tall with hard long eyes
> as she stands,with her long hard hands keeping
> silence on her dress,good for sleeping
> is her long hard body filled with surprise
> like a white shocking wire,when she smiles
> a hard long smile it sometimes makes
> gaily go clean through me tickling aches,
> and the weak noise of her eyes easily files
> my impatience to an edge—my girl's tall
> and taut,with thin legs just like a vine
> that's spent all of its life on a garden-wall,
> and is going to die. When we grimly go to bed
> with these legs she begins to heave and twine
> about me,and to kiss my face and head.
>
> (*CP,* 133)

Other examples from this period used the rhyme scheme of the sonnet loosely and did not even provide the sufficient number of syllables
per line for pentameter—and, what is more, sometimes arbitrarily
pushed the words about on the page, as in this poem describing a
French prostitute lying in bed in her gaslit room, which is decorated
with a crucifix:

the bed is not very big

a sufficient pillow shoveling
her small manure-shaped head

one sheet on which distinctly wags

at times the weary twig
of a neckless nudity
(very occasionally budding

a flabby algebraic odour

jigs
        et tout en face
always wiggles the perfectly dead
finger of thitherhithering gas.

clothed with a luminous fur

poilu

        a Jesus sags
in frolicsome wooden agony).

                                        (*CP*, 207)

   Besides violating literary tradition in this sonnet, Cummings pro-
ferred not only a literary outrage to womanhood in the metaphor of the
street-sweeper shoveling up horse-droppings but also an effront to religion by viewing the crucifixion as "frolicsome."
   If at times ugliness or deliberate attempts to shock prevail, at other
times wit or hard-edged humor predominate, as in this sonnet in which
Cummings oscillates between slang and Latinate diction:

        twentyseven bums give a prostitute the once
        -over. fiftythree(and one would see if it could)

        eyes say the breasts look very good:
        firmlysquirmy with a slight jounce,

        thirteen pants have a hunch

admit in threedimensional distress
these hips were made for Horizontal Business
(set on big legs nice to pinch

assiduously which justgraze
each other). As the lady lazily struts
                                                              (her
thickish flesh superior to the genuine daze
of unmarketable excitation,

whose careless movements carefully scatter

pink propaganda of annihilation

                                                              (*CP,* 130)

Here phrases like "the once-over" and "have a hunch" bounce off of
mathematical circumlocutions such as "threedimensional distress" and
"Horizontal Business." This juxtaposition only gives effervescence to the
broad humor already present in the use of the venerable sonnet form for
this scene of indigent ogling.

Another sonnet, one that marks Cummings' farewell to Cambridge, is
technically more sophisticated in the way he works in phrases that the
gossipy ladies might let drop and a question that implies they have no
idea of what charitable causes they worked for. He satirizes closed minds
filled with attitudes that have been handed down to them in the way
that a "Furnished Room" will have used, worn furniture that does not fit
well together in its shabby clutter:

the Cambridge ladies who live in furnished souls
are unbeautiful and have comfortable minds
(also,with the church's protestant blessings
daughters,unscented shapeless spirited)
they believe in Christ and Longfellow,both dead,
are invariably interested in so many things—
at the present writing one still finds
delighted fingers knitting for the is it Poles?
perhaps. While permanent faces coyly bandy
scandal of Mrs. N and Professor D
. . . . the Cambridge ladies do not care,above
Cambridge if sometimes in its box of
sky lavender and cornerless,the
moon rattles like a fragment of angry candy

                                                              (*CP,* 115)

The final simile is a stroke of surprise that would have pleased T. E. Hulme. The Cambridge ladies cannot respond to beauty: to them the moon is like the last stale chocolate that no one wants and is left in the box.

In other poems sound-patterns govern the presentation. In the following poem Cummings shows how he had learned to take a subject associated with ugliness and sordidness and, using alliteration, consonance, and internal rhyme, create an aesthetic complex:

between the breasts
of bestial
Marj lie large
men who praise

Marj's cleancornered strokable
body        these men's
fingers toss trunks
shuffle sacks spin kegs they

curl
loving
around
beers

   the world has
these men's hands but their
bodies big and boozing
belong to

Marj
the greenslim purse of whose
face opens
on a fatgold

grin
hooray
hoorah for the large
men who lie

between the breasts
of bestial Marj
for the strong men
who

sleep between the legs of Lil

(*CP*, 85)

Repetition of consonant sound always provides auditory pleasure, but Cummings takes advantage of other effects that it also can bring about. The "b" sounds of "between the breasts" draw the meanings of the two words together, so that the "between"-ness of the men's position is emphasized. Alliteration can also heighten contrast in meaning or connotation: the word "bestial" following "breasts" is jarring. Cummings can pull the reader back and forth, as here in the attractiveness of the sexual pleasure suddenly halted by the repulsion from sexual intercourse with someone "bestial." As the poem develops, however, the emphasis on the physicality of the men's daily work makes the sex with Marj appropriate, especially when their daily work is described in pleasing patterns of alliterative sound: "toss trunks/ shuffle sacks spin kegs." The description that follows of their moments of relaxation then softens the whole transaction with Marj: the mellifluous consonance of the "l" and "r" sounds and the long vowel sounds, "curl/ loving/ around/ beers," brings this about. Again the "b" sounds draw together and intensify meaning so that the "belong"-ingness of the "bodies big and boozing" is reinforced. The poem ends with the introduction of another prostitute, "Lil," whose alliterating "legs" invite the "strong" men's alliterating "sleep." Although the attitude of the speaker seems at first to be condescending, this notion is dispelled by the time we reach the direct assertion of the joy of sexual pleasure celebrated in the "hooray/ hoorah" for the "large men" who "lie" with Marj—which is in the same spirit as the soul of the speaker that "Hollers" with the joy of spring.

Cummings had been developing what I call his Satyric style, which is, as my spelling suggests, a means to express libidinous energy as well as to criticize follies and evils. Its range is extreme. At the low or naturalistic end of the scale it implies a rejection of life or society and often takes the form of ugliness. At the upper end of the scale wit and high spirits indulge in mockery and making fun of human follies. This lighter vein is most evident in the early part of Cummings' career. It directs our attention to pompous, stupid, hypocritical, or mendacious people and the high and low places in which they can be found. As Cummings continued to write and publish he used the Satyric style more and more frequently to attack professors, politicians, salesmen, generals, businessmen, and national leaders. If the style is in any way mythical it is so in its demonic approach, for it reflects a dark view of human behavior and a hostile attitude toward society. We shall see this side of Cummings' outlook coming forward more prominently in the later part of his career.

## III

Simultaneously with the creation of these poems bristling with harsh worldly detail, Cummings was composing work that moved in the opposite, although equally revolutionary, direction. This time it was his contact with European art that made the difference. The year following his graduation from Harvard had carried him into the milieu of writing and painting in New York City's Greenwich Village, where there was a budding interest in the new movements in European art. Then during the war he had been exposed to the modern movement in music, set design, ballet, painting, and sculpture in Paris, where he had gone to performances of Les Ballets Russes and seen Stravinsky's *Petrouchka* twice. He had seen the premiere performance of Erik Satie's *Parade* with Cubist sets by Picasso. He had absorbed the glories of Impressionist painting in the Luxembourg Museum. And, of course, he had not forgotten the work of Duchamp-Villon and Brancusi at the Armory Show. By 1918 he was no longer just an observer or an awed responder to the art scene: he had been working as a Cubist painter for several months.

This turmoil of influences was bound to sweep Cummings beyond the experiments he had been carrying out in 1916. Now at Camp Devens he plunged into language with a determination to be part of the twentieth-century revolution in the arts. "The symbol of all art is the Prism," he jotted in his notes. "The goal is unrealism. The method is destructive. To break up the white light of objective realism into the secret glories which it contains."[7]

One way to do it was to mix the arts together, as in the poem in which Cummings expresses himself as an experiential being in the process of becoming formed, as if an artwork were being created. The technique is synaesthetic: action and speech are rendered in terms of color:

> my mind is
> a big hunk of irrevocable nothing which touch and taste and smell
> and hearing and sight keep hitting and chipping with sharp fatal
> tools
> in an agony of sensual chisels i perform squirms of chrome and ex-
> ecute strides of cobalt
> nevertheless i
> feel that i cleverly am being altered that i slightly am becoming
> something a little different,in fact
> myself
> Hereupon helpless i utter lilac shreiks and scarlet bellowings.
>
> (*CP*, 97)

In another poem he describes what his psyche has become as if it were a Postimpressionist painting.

> of my
> soul a street is:
> prettinesses Pic-
> abian tricktrickclickflick-er
> garnished
> of stark Picasso
> throttling trees
>
> hither
> my soul
> repairs herself with
> prisms of sharp mind
> and Matisse rhythms
> to juggle Kandinsky gold-fish
>
> away from the gripping gigantic
> muscles of Cézanne's
> logic,
>      oho.
>      a street
> there is
>
> where strange birds      purr

*(CP, 69)*

Here the technique is allusive, but he attempts to help the reader out by conveying his own sense of Picabian repetitiveness, Picasso's spare lines (rendered in angles resulting from the dividing and rearranging of reality by "prisms of sharp mind"), the dance of Matisse's curves, the color movement of Kandinsky's abstraction, and the strength of Cézanne's orderliness. The result is a new world where creatures are merged into something new: "strange birds purr."

At the time of the false armistice in November 1918 Cummings tried expressing the confusions of the celebration in a long poem called "NOISE." This is an extract:

> thugs of clumsy mutter shove upward leaving fat
>      feet-prints,rumbles poke buzzing thumbs
>      in eye of world

> stovelike emotion rapidly scrambles toots and
>       scurry nibbling screams and sleek
>       whistles which sprint ribbons of
>       white shriek! . . .
>
> Wall Street wriggles choked with gesturing
>       human swill squirms gagged with
>       a sprouting filth of faces extra!
>       PEACE millions like crabs about a
>
> prosperous penis of bigness the woolworth
>       building,slowly waving
>
>                                   (*CP*, 951–52)

The expressive aim was to melt together impressions of sight and sound and to make nonsensical joinings of mismatched nouns and adjectives with illogical verbs in order to convey the unruly jubilance, the crowds, and the hullabaloo. It was not successful; he put the poem aside. His Cubist poem "writhe and" had been a striking achievement two years earlier, but not all of his trials could come up to that level.

This second kind of Cummings poem from this era falls into another stylistic category that I call Hephaestian, after the Greek god of the forge, because in work like this the poet was bending, breaking, twisting, mending, and reshaping materials in order to create new forms of literary expression.[8] He was incorporating the new artistic spirit of Paris into his poetic technique in order to develop this Hephaestian style, which may be described as using elliptical statement, fragmented expression, images that surprise and juxtapositions that shock, wrenchings and distortions of diction, and in general, violations of expectation in linguistic usage. "Picasso" is one of the most successful works in this style. The poem is a tribute to the artist in language that expresses a response to his achievement and suggests the manner in which he achieved it: the sculptural dimension of his Cubist technique, the clash of intersecting planes, and the intellectuality of his approach:

> Picasso
> you give us Things
> which
> bulge:grunting lungs pumped full of sharp thick mind

The "Things" (capitalized for emphasis)—general artistic products, not paintings—"which/bulge" are palpable, suggesting tactile surfaces with additional dimensions. Picasso's work thrusts forth a complex vitality, having the full breath of life as well as intellectual vigor ("sharp thick mind"), and plenty of it ("pumped full"), its sharpness and thickness reinforcing the idea of the palpable.

> you make us shrill
> presents always
> shut in the sumptuous screech of
> simplicity

A sound motif is initiated now—"shrill," "screech"—which will later echo in such words as "squeak," "squeals," "shrieking," and "screams," all of which convey the sense of piercing sound. But the idea of a disciplining enclosure ("shut") brings control, and the effect is one of richness in frugality ("sumptuous" and "simplicity").

> out of the
> black unbunged
> Something gushes vaguely a squeak of planes
> or
>
> between squeals of
> Nothing grabbed with circular shrieking tightness
> solid screams whisper

Earlier motifs are reiterated and begin to intermix with newer ones. The "Thing" is seen to have both an energy ("Something") and an absence ("Nothing"); the sharpness reappears in "planes"; but the containment ("circular") is drawn into a "tightness" and, similarly, the piercing sounds are concentrated in "whisper" in the same way the palpability is pulled together into "solid." All of these paradoxical mergers and formal controls of erupting sounds and centrifugal forces describe the artistic product. Then a new metaphor for the artist is added, a lumberjack, a sculptor of nature (Did Cummings have in mind Picasso's *La Grande Dryade* of 1908?), whose territory lies within self:

Lumberman of the Distinct

your brain's
axe only chops hugest inherent
Trees of Ego,from

whose living and biggest
bodies lopped
of every
prettiness

you hew form truly

(*CP*, 95)

This poem does not have much visually directive spacing, but it does employ the Cubist devices of startling juxtapositions and compressed associations. Cummings called these effects of interplay and conflict between words and their appropriate realms of meaning "the Rhythm of Sense." When he combined this procedure with the manipulation of words on the page he was exhibiting the outstanding feature of twentieth-century art, the process of "breakup and restructuring." For example, a Cubist painting is something like a cut-up photograph whose pieces have been rearranged, or it is like a subject broken out of a two-dimensional framework and shown from several angles at once. Or, to take an example from prose fiction, an avant-garde novel may be one in which the time-scheme has been broken up and certain fragments rearranged to become the completed whole. With work of the sort that he had been developing since 1916 Cummings had become a valid representative of the new analytical technique in the arts.

By 1919 he had compiled a manuscript for a volume of poems that he called "Tulips & Chimneys."[9] But publishers are wary of radically different voices when they first emerge in the literary scene. Four years were to pass before even a selection of these poems that challenged poetic conventions would appear in a truncated version of the original collection. By that time even the title had lost its ampersand, to be replaced by a more acceptable "and."

Meanwhile the first book of Cummings' to find its way to publication turned out to be a volume not of poetry, but prose—or something like prose.

# Chapter Four
## The Enormous Room

E. E. Cummings wanted to be a painter-poet, and after the war was over his double career was showing some promise. His poems had begun to appear in the *Dial* as well as in other avant-garde magazines—the *Liberator, Broom, Secession,* and *S4N.* He was able to have a couple of paintings hung each year in the annual exhibitions of the New York Society of Independent Artists. But his talents received their first widespread recognition with the publication of an autobiographical narrative, *The Enormous Room* (1922), about his experiences during the war in a French detention camp, and this came about by chance rather than by his own choosing.

When Estlin had returned to the United States after that ordeal, his father urged him to write an account of his imprisonment because he intended to sue the French government and thought it would provide strong evidence to support a lawsuit. Estlin was reluctant to do so and went back to his painting and poetry. But then Edward Cummings offered him $1000 if he would carry out the task. On the condition that it not be used for a lawsuit Estlin finally agreed, partly for the money and partly to please his father.

Cummings' decision occurred at a time when there was a thriving market for the works of journalists, novelists, and poets revealing the realities of the Great War. During the war itself the prevailing publications were patriotic in tone, as seen in books such as Arthur Guy Empey's *Over the Top,* Richard Harding Davis's *With the Allies,* and in the poems of Alan Seeger and Rupert Brooke, or were serious historical analyses of the causes of the war, such as Fredrick Scott Oliver's *Ordeal by Battle.* But as soon as 1918, the disillusionment with the war and its aims had set in. Philip Gibbs published *Now It Can Be Told,* about the horrors of the Western Front; John Reed had brought out *Ten Days That Shook the World,* about the breakdown of the Russian army on the Eastern Front and the ensuing revolution; Sigfried Sassoon had published both Wilfred Owen's poems and his own volumes, *Counter Attack* and *War Poems,* with their antiwar themes. Cummings' friend John Dos Passos had already published two antiwar novels, *One Man's Initiation—1917* and *Three Soldiers*.[1]

Thus the wide reception of Cummings' *The Enormous Room* was partly due to its being an exposé of the harshness and injustice of the French government toward aliens during the war. Yet Cummings' book made more than a contemporary splash; it has gone through many editions and has never been out of print. The lasting value of the work has to do with Cummings' linguistic and mythic handling of his materials.

The factual bases of the narrative can be summarized quickly. Cummings describes the way in which he and his friend William Slater Brown were arrested on false charges of espionage because Brown had written letters to friends in the United States expressing pacifist views and giving reports of the dispirited morale of the French troops.[2] They were hauled before an investigative board in Noyon, where Cummings, who had nothing to do with the letters, refused to say that he hated the Germans and declared only that he loved the French. Even so, on the grounds that he was Brown's accomplice, he was sent to the Dépôt de Triage at La Ferté-Macé, a small town west of Paris, where he remained for four months until his father obtained his release through the American embassy. The Dépôt was a three-building complex, formerly a seminary, in which the men were housed in a huge gymnasium-like room. The inmates were a curious mixture of international misfits: petty criminals, soldiers who had overstayed their leave, merchant-marine sailors who had missed the departure of their ships, and aliens whose presence in France worried the French authorities. Also held in one of the buildings were a large number of women, mostly prostitutes who were arrested for plying their trade too close to the front lines.

Cummings' book is a detailed account, of his experiences at this detention center falling into three parts.[3] Part I tells of his arrest and his three days of travel, escorted by gendarmes, to Ferté-Macé. Part II describes the conditions there, the daily schedule, and the behavior of the administrators and guards. It also offers an extensive series of portraits of the detainees, most of whom became friends of Cummings and of Brown, who had preceded Cummings to the Dépôt. Part III covers the final days of confinement. After being interrogated by a security commission Brown was sent to a French prison and the despondent Cummings fell into a depressed state until, shortly afterward, he was freed and sent back first to Paris and then the United States.

11. CUMMINGS IN FRANCE
WITH THE NORTON-
HARJES AMBULANCE CORPS.
COMIC PENCIL SKETCH OF
HIMSELF AT GERMAINE,
1917.
*Courtesy of the Houghton Library,
Harvard University*

For his book Cummings, who was fully familiar with how Joyce had used Homer's *Odyssey* as a framing device for his novel *Ulysses,* chose John Bunyan's *Pilgrim's Progress* as his structural myth. Bunyan's Pilgrim, crying, "Life, life, eternal life," had set out on an allegorical journey to the Celestial City and after many adventures, including his fall into the Slough of Despond, his capture by the Giant Despair, and his battle with the fiendish angel Apollyon (Satan), had passed through the Delectable Mountains to reach his final destination. Cummings' use of allusions to Bunyan's allegory gives an extra dimension to his narrative as well as a push toward universality. Although there are not many direct correspondences, the reader who is familiar with Bunyan's work will perceive that La Boue Héroïque (the epic mud) at the ambulance unit's station is the Slough of Despond, the harsh Directeur of the Dépôt is Apollyon, Cummings' depression after Brown's departure intimates his capture by the Giant Despair, the four inmates most admired by Cummings represent the Delectable Mountains, and his arrival at Paris and finally New York corresponds to the achievement of the Celestial City. Enduring his captivity becomes the pilgrimage of the narrator and his progress is the testing process that causes him to understand the meaning of the war, the nature of authority, the responses of oppressed human beings, and the preciousness of individual life and freedom.

The antiwar themes were the most readily apparent to Cummings' readers in the 1920s. He ridicules all the phrases that the Allies used to color the war with grandiose purpose, such as "The Great War for Humanity," (146) "La Gloire and Le Patriotisme" (123). He mocks the rhetoric of "Our Great President": "the saving of civilization from the clutches of Prussian tyranny" (3). He wonders perhaps if the schoolmaster has been imprisoned because he told "the children that there were such monstrous things as peace and good will" (119). He includes a revelation by a French detainee that the soldiers on leave deliberately get venereal disease so that they could escape duty at the front. He records anecdotes told by Belgian inmates of the superiority of German prison conditions and of the ready payment by German soldiers for anything taken from Belgian villagers. He admires Surplice, one of the Delectable Mountains, because he does not know that there is a war taking place and because he cannot conceive of such a thing as a submarine.

His whole treatment of the war is topsy-turvy. He has a comic-opera description of the German scout aircraft that fly over Paris and of all the French antiaircraft guns that go off together "for the sake of sympathy." His arrest is a joyous occasion because he is getting away from the ambulance corps where he and Brown were in constant contention with their commander. He feels completely happy the first time he is held in a jail cell. He and Brown think that La Ferté-Macé is "the finest place on earth" because of their fascinating companions.

Besides the antidote to patriotic accounts of the war Cummings reveals in *The Enormous Room* a personal theme of hostility to authority, which extends itself to being antigovernment. This attitude toward authority, which had its beginnings in his late adolescence as rebellion against his father, had been fully nourished at La Ferté-Macé and at Camp Devens, and it remained with him the rest of his life in fully developed form. The book is laced through with denunciations, both direct and ironic, against le gouvernement français. He rejoices in having suspected traitors as friends. He compares the mistreatment of prisoners at La Ferté-Macé with the U.S. government's handling of conscientious objectors. The conflict with authority reaches its peak in a passage threatening and predicting the revolution of the weak and helpless in the overthrow of oppressive governmental structures. (Cummings was bla-

12. DÉPÔT DE TRIAGE AT LA FERTÉ-MACÉ. THE ENORMOUS ROOM WAS
ON THE TOP FLOOR OF THE BUILDING ON THE LEFT. THE CHAPEL IS
THE BUILDING ON THE RIGHT.

tantly alluding to the Russian Revolution.) What gives rise to this out-
burst is a fierce statement about the self-deifying arrogance of the ruling
figures who are indifferent to the sufferings of the poor, as personified in
the little Machine Fixer, a five-foot Belgian with a crippled arm.
Cummings then offers this apostrophe: "O gouvernement français,I
think it was not very clever of you to put this terrible doll in La Ferté;I
should have left him in Belgium with his little doll-wife if I had been
You;for when Governments are found dead there is always a little doll on
top of them,pulling and tweaking with his little hands to get back the
microscopic knife which sticks firmly in the quiet meat of their hearts"
(103). This opposition to authority is related to Cummings' hostility
toward civilization *per se,* a feature of the Romantic individualism that he
had worked out for himself as a philosophy of life. Romantic individualism pervades all of Cummings' subsequent work, although it is less evident in the earlier poems than in those of the 1930s and after. It is given
its first full treatment in *The Enormous Room.*

Cummings' Romantic outlook gives value to feeling over thinking,
respects the natural life rather than the civilized life, admires untutored
ignorance more than education, and sees the behavior of children as infi-
nitely superior to that of mature human beings. It is the kind of
Romanticism we find in Wordsworth as well as in Mark Twain. As for
the individualism, it is premised on the recognition that every human
being is unique and that to express that uniqueness is the fulfillment of
personality and the most important achievement any person can carry

out in life. Conversely, to conform to the behavior of the group or to the rules of society is to suppress that essential self and thus to fail at living and to forfeit one's right to respect.

In many of his notes and in his essay on Gaston Lachaise,[4] Cummings presents his theory metaphorically using both organic and grammatical terms: to be unique is to be alive, and thus the "Verb" represents that vitality; the opposite is to be dead to life, to be a "Noun"—something that has stopped growing, that has no "kinesis," no movement. Forms of the verb "to be" best convey individuality: "I am" expresses uniqueness; an uninhibited, unrepressed human being is an "Is." Such an explanation can make clear an otherwise obscure passage in *The Enormous Room:* "There are certain things in which one is unable to believe for the simple reason that he never ceases to feel them. Things of this sort—things which are always inside of us and in fact are us and which consequently will not be pushed off or away where we can begin thinking about them—are no longer things;they,and the us which they are,equals A Verb; an IS" (168). The autobiographical narrative *The Enormous Room* presents these ideas in action.

The subtext of *The Enormous Room* is the revelation of the narrator as someone fulfilling his reason for existence. He is the Romantic individualist. His arrest becomes paradoxically a release into freedom. As a result it provides him with an experience of joy in being alive; he is freed from the oppressive forces that surrounded him in his ambulance corps unit. When he is taken to spend the night in jail at nearby Noyon, his first response as the cell door slams behind him is telling: "I put the bed-roll down. I stood up. I was myself. An uncontrollable joy gutted me after three months of humiliation, of being bossed and herded and bullied and insulted. I was myself and my own master" (17). Although he is confined in a cell that has only one tiny window high up on the wall, that is filled with the stink from the unclean toilet can, and whose walls are covered with the despairing graffiti of former prisoners, he revels in his new experience. He whistles and sings; he composes a poem that he scratches on the wall with burnt matches; he feeds a piece of chocolate to a mouse; and he goes to sleep enjoying the beams of moonlight coming through his window slot and feeling one with the cosmos.

When he is interrogated by a trio of French security police he refuses to disassociate himself from his friend Brown and rejects their persuasions to denounce the Germans even though he knows that it could mean the lifting of charges against him. At La Ferté-Macé, he takes immense pleasure in his new and unusual companions. He and Brown give them all identifying labels—The Machine Fixer,

Garibaldi, The Bear, the Orange Cap, Bathhouse John, and so on. His appreciation of these unique individuals is in inverse proportion to their education and sophistication. His favorites are ignorant, illiterate, and naive, but capable of expressing their feelings truly and without restraint.

Outstanding are the four he designates as the Delectable Mountains: the Wanderer, a gypsy who is utterly devoted to his wife and child (incarcerated in nearby quarters) and who can weep profusely at the memory of the forced sale of his horse; Zulu, a Pole who can speak neither French nor English but who can communicate completely by means of facial expression and body language; Surplice, a dirty, happy, unobtrusive vagrant who is the butt of everyone's jokes and derision ("of nobody can he say My Friend, of no one has he ever said or will ever say My Enemy," 186) and who can draw heavenly music from a mere harmonica; and Jean Le Negre, "a pillar of strutting muscle," noisy, laughing, joking, posturing, who has the mind of a child. "Of all the fine people in La Ferté-Macé," says Cummings, "Monsieur Jean . . . swaggers in my memory as the finest" (198).

All these people are "Alive," and they respond fully to the friendship of Cummings and Brown. Because of their unsullied ignorance they can appreciate an artistic project of Cummings', namely, the making of a color chart by means of pieces of tin foil, bits of cloth, leaves, cigarette-box wrappers, and other debris. Because they help him collect these materials their participation allows Cummings to make the single statement in the book that relates art to his Romantic view of life. He contrasts his newly made friends with the Great American Public whose response to art is inhibited by education: "Let no one sound his indignant yawp at this. I refer to the fact that,for an educated gent or lady,to create is first of all to destroy—that there is and can be no such thing as authentic art until the *bons trucs* (whereby we are taught to see and imitate on canvas and in stone and by words this so-called world) are entirely and thoroughly and perfectly annihilated by that vast and painful process of Unthinking which may result in a minute bit of purely personal Feeling. Which minute bit is Art" (224).

But besides the view of life that is articulated in the book it is Cummings' use of language that makes it so completely his own. It is written in what linguisticians would call his idiolect—that is, his own personal way with words. In straight narration he says very little in a way that conforms to the norms of expression. He states what he has to say on a low colloquial level, and even in slang, or in a highly stylized formal diction that mocks its subject. Moreover, since the action takes place in France, he offers a macaronic mix of American English sprinkled with French phrases or dialogue. Sometimes he even translates French words or phrases into English literally in order to give a foreign flavor to the narration: the cook sent men to "seek water" or to "catch water"; the work crew that carried the slop pails down from the Room "descended the excrement"; when all the prisoners climbed the stairs to the dining area "the world mounted." Occasionally he even intrudes a bit of Chaucerian English: for example, when the Inspector does not understand the full import of what his prisoner is saying Cummings phrases it thus: "but that was something which pauvre M. le Surveillant wot altogether not of" (83).

In addition Cummings has his own adjectival idiosyncrasies: a door can be "crisp," a darkness is "gruesomely tactile," the priest is a "strangely soggy creature." In conveying his experience he will sometimes suggest the bewilderment that he felt by using an impressionistic style—that is, he records images, without explanation, in the way that they would fall on the consciousness of a perceiver. For instance, his glimpse in the jail at Gré of an animated crowd of prisoners is suddenly flashed this way: "A wall with many bars fixed across one minute opening. At the opening a dozen,fifteen,grins. Upon the bars,hands scraggy and bluishly white. Through the bars stretchings of lean arms,incessant stretchings. The grins leap at the window,hands belonging to them catch hold,arms belonging to the hands stretch in my direction—an instant;then new grins leap from behind and knock off the first grins which go down with a fragile crashing like glass smashed:hands wither and break,arms streak out of sight,sucked inward" (26). When he extends this kind of locution further it becomes what may be called "cubist" prose—that is, having jarring juxtapositions, wrenched phrases, surprising epithets. This style can be seen, for example, in a passage that describes a group of Algerians waiting for a train who take a drunken friend to a nearby spot to rest:

> The drunk was accordingly escorted into the dark,his friends'
> abrupt steps correcting his large slovenly procedure,out of
> earshot—Some of the Black People sat down near me,and
> smoked. Their enormous faces, wads of vital darkness, swooped
> with fatigue. Their vast gentle hands lay noisily about their knees.
>     The departed gendarmes returned with a bump,out of the
> mist. The train for Paris would arrive *de suite*. . . . Then with the
> ghostly miniature roar of an insane toy the train for Paris came
> fumbling cautiously into the station. (29)

This unabashed play with language can be disconcerting to the reader at first, but soon we get used to it in the same way that we adjust to any unusual person's idiolect. We can then find it successful in expressing a diversity of effects—amusement, irony, indignation, excitement, and even pathos.

It is this combination of fresh and challenging language and an intensely personal view of life that has kept *The Enormous Room* in print for over seven decades. It is like no other war memoir; it is unlike any tale of capture and release. It has often been called a novel, but it is not fiction—it is instead a story couched in such unorthodox language, from witty to sentimental, from lyric exultation to frothing denunciation, that it defies classification.

## Chapter Five
# Tulips, Chimneys, &

Sometime in 1919 Cummings had assembled a hefty manuscript of poems entitled "Tulips & Chimneys," which he gave to his friend Stewart Mitchell, the managing editor of the *Dial,* asking him to help find a publisher. Mitchell tried six publishing houses without success. Cummings then removed some of the poems that an editor might find either unpoetic or obscene, rearranged their order, and tried again in 1922, through John Dos Passos, to find a home for his wayweary volume. This 1922 collection of 152 poems eventually saw publication, but not all at once. Dos Passos managed to persuade Thomas Seltzer to publish a selection of sixty-six of the poems under the title *Tulips and Chimneys* in 1923. (Cummings was furious that Seltzer did not use the ampersand in the title.) Lincoln MacVeagh of the Dial Press made another selection from what was left over and published *XLI Poems* in 1925. What the two editors avoided were the most experimental as well as the most sexually daring of the poems. Cummings was thus reduced to venturing a private publication with the items that remained, to whose company he restored some of the poems he had withdrawn in 1922, and to which he also added a few more pieces he had written when he returned to Paris in 1921. He called the volume *&* (his ampersand at last dignified into a title) and brought it forth early in 1925.

If Cummings' first version, "Tulips & Chimneys," had been put before the public in 1919 it would have established, four years earlier, his place in the twentieth-century revolution in literature. It is now possible to see what such a volume would have been like because George Firmage reconstructed and published the 1922 version in 1976. Since this edition represents the stage of development that Cummings had reached by 1919, we should consider its contents in close detail.

The first portion, "Tulips," contains an immense variety of Cummings' earlier work, including poems that had appeared in the *Harvard Monthly;* poems that he had written for Dean Briggs in classroom assignments; a long Hellenistic "Epithalamion" that he had composed for Scofield Thayer's wedding; a long tribute ("Puella Mea") to Elaine Thayer, Scofield's wife, with whom he had fallen in love; and a

13. PENCIL SKETCH OF HIS ROOM IN THE HOTEL ST. ANDRÉ
DES ARTS, PARIS, 1922, BY E. E. CUMMINGS.
*Courtesy of the Houghton Library, Harvard University*

Keatsian fantasy inspired by *Aucassin and Nicolette.* This early work, which was divided into the categories "Songs," "Chansons Innocentes" (which contained "in Just-" and "Tumbling-hair"), "Orientale," and "Amores," is, for the most part, a series of free-verse exercises traditional in tone. The only Cummings touch that adds distinction is his manipulation of typography through lowercase and capital letters and his play with spacing. Two of these early poems give evidence that even his classroom exercises disclose a true poetic voice. One is a genuinely singable lyric that begins "when god lets my body be/ From each brave eye shall sprout a tree" and ends "and all the while shall my heart be/ With the bulge and nuzzle of the sea" (*CP,* 19). The other is a ballad-like piece in the medieval manner that begins

> All in green went my love riding
> on a great horse of gold
> into the silver dawn.
>
> four lean hounds crouched low and smiling
> the merry deer ran before.
>
> Fleeter be they than dappled dreams
> the swift sweet deer
> the red rare deer.
>
> Four red roebuck at a white water
> the cruel bugle sang before . . .
>
> (*CP,* 15)

Then comes a more untraditional series of poems grouped under the headings "La Guerre," "Impressions," "Portraits," and "Post Impressions." By their references to both modern music and painting, the categories thus far suggest a mixture of the arts, and one can sense the presence of Debussy, Monet, and Cézanne even in the table of contents. The "Impressions" are, appropriately, descriptive poems, usually with an emphasis on light. The especially delicate "Impression II" uses the metaphor of piano-playing to carry the image of springtime rain before it changes into mist and fog:

> the sky a silver
> dissonance by the correct
> fingers of April
> resolved
>
>         into a
> clutter of trite jewels
>
>
> now like a moth with stumbling

                    wings flutters and flops along the
                    grass collides with trees and
                    houses and finally,
                    butts into the river

                                                                    (*CP,* 60)

But death still intrudes upon some of these renderings of the diurnal
variations of light, as in the opening lines of "Impressions IX":

        The hours rise up putting off stars and it is
        dawn
        into the street of the sky light walks scattering poems

        on earth a candle is
        extinguished        the city
        wakes
        with a song upon her
        mouth having death in her eyes

        and it is dawn
        the world
        goes forth to murder dreams . . .

                                                                    (*CP,* 67)

Among the "Portraits," along with "bestial Marj," we have several
representations of the seamy side of life expressed in the Satyric style: a
drunken woman passed out on the sidewalk ("the/ nimble/ heat"); a
street evangelist ("the skinny voice"); a grubby Greek restaurant ("it's
just like a coffin's/ inside when you die"); a family in an ugly street scene
("i walked the boulevard"); a prostitute in monologue ("raise the shade/
will youse dearie"); five men in a Middle Eastern café ("5/ derbies-with-
men-in-them smoke Helmar"), and so on. The settings are frequently
crowded with repellent detail. This nightclub scene is representative:

            between nose-red gross
            walls      sprawling with tipsy
            tables the abominable
            floor belches smoky

            laughter into the filagree
            frame of a microscopic
            stage whose jouncing curtain.      ,rises
            upon one startling doll . . .

                                                                    (*CP,* 80)

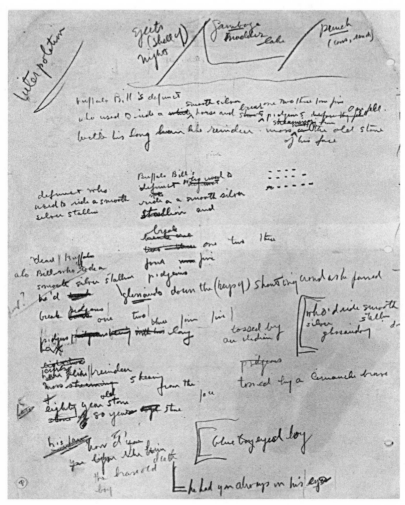

**14. NOTES AND DRAFTS FOR "BUFFALO BILL'S," JANUARY 1917**
*Courtesy of the Houghton Library, Harvard University*

Yet the metaphorical language here compresses the features and actions of drunks into the description of the scene, and the handling of the punctuation suggests the motion of the curtain—so that an aesthetic complex begins to form. Thus in spite of all the repulsiveness we are getting genuine free-verse poems in this section. Moreover, Buffalo Bill and Picasso appear as a couple of bright spots among the "Portraits."

Next come the "Post Impressions." As they begin we look at the natural scene again—the sunset, a seascape, cloud cover, and so on—but the forcing of language and the jumbled typography now take us to the far edge of expression. For example, in "Post Impressions II" we are buffeted with the Hephaestian style as adjectives are mismatched with their nouns:

> beyond the brittle towns asleep
> i look where stealing needles of foam
> in the last light
>
> thread the creeping shores
>
>
> as out of dumb strong hands infinite
>
> the erect deep upon me
> in the last light
> pours its eyeless miles
>
>
> the chattering sunset ludicrously
> dies,i hear only tidewings
>
> in the last light
> twitching at the world

(CP, 104)

Yet sometimes, when it is dealing with an appropriate subject, the style can soothe, as in the poem entitled "SNO," which carries metaphors of cleansing and of gentle, scarcely perceptible sounds of falling snowflakes:

a white idea (Listen

drenches:earth's ugly)mind.
,Rinsing with exact death

the annual brain
                    clotted with loosely voices
look
look.    Skilfully

.fingered by(a parenthesis
the)pond on whoseswooning edge

black trees think
(hear little knives of flower
stropping sof a.    Thick silence)

blacktreesthink
tiny,angels sharpen:themselves
(on
     air)
don't speak
                    A white idea,

drenching.     earth's brain detaches
clottingsand from a a nnual(ugliness
of)rinsed mind slowly:

from!the:A wending putrescence.    a.of,loosely


;voices
                                        (*CP*, 113)


　　　Images, space, and oddities of punctuation combine to develop a
snowfall breathlessly heard rather than depicted. Color and concept
merge in the image of the snow; then the command to "Listen" is suddenly intruded. The space that follows here and elsewhere in the poem
allows, each time, for quiet to prevail. The "drenching" of earth makes it
a wet snowfall and thus able to do the "Rinsing." Earth is given a "mind"
for the "idea" to cleanse, but its brain is only annual and thus comes to

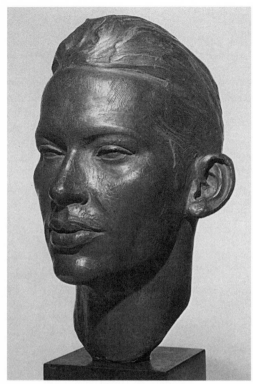

15. BRONZE BUST OF
CUMMINGS BY GASTON
LACHAISE, 1927.
*Courtesy of the Fogg Art Museum,
Harvard University Art
Museums. Bequest of Marion M.
Cummings*

death in the natural cycle because it has become "clotted." The
snowflakes, "loosely" falling, that bring the cleansing death are now
"voices" that we have been asked to listen for. The period and the
comma are presumably other pauses for listening. Then we are com-
manded to "look" and perceive that the earth is touched ("fingered") by
a pond, where the snow is melting ("swooning") and where the contrast-
ing black of the trees is another concept. Now new sound metaphors are
introduced: snowflakes as flower petals gently sliding over a razorstrop
or as angel feathers. Repetition of the command for silence and the
metaphor of the "white idea" cleansing the earth now lead to the visual
breakup of words and intrusions of punctuation marks to suggest the
dissolving of the clotted brain and an image of a muddy stream of melt-
ed snow ("A wending putrescence") winding into the pond.

    There are troubles in expression however. The illogical adjective
"exact" has, by now, been so overused by Cummings that it has become

a hackneyed term in his poetic vocabulary. The "(a parenthesis/ the)" device is an arbitrary item of logographic teasing. In his experiments with expression Cummings can be careless in his early work.

But among the "Post Impressions" we also have glimpses of the human scene, especially in three prose-poems (forms that Cummings learned from Mallarmé and Rimbaud) about an organ grinder and his monkey, about the rush hour in lower Manhattan, and about McSorley's saloon on the lower East Side. The last is especially notable in its attempt to create a collage of sound. What the poem presents in this vignette is a suggestion of evil as it makes its appearance in a bar-room. But of greatest interest is Cummings' play with words that have rhyme and consonance—*dint, grin, point, glint, squint,* and *wink*—or words that begin or end with similar consonant sounds—*piddle, spittle, topple, dribble, gobble.* In addition there is a collage of onomatopoeic bar-room sounds mixed with snippets of the customers' talk. We might call this work a sound painting. Here is an excerpt from the opening of the piece:

i was sitting in mcsorley's.       outside it was New York and beautifully snowing.

Inside snug and evil.       the slobbering walls filthily push witless
creases of screaming warmth chuck pillows are noise funnily swallows
swallowing revolvingly pompous a the swallowed mottle with smooth or
a but of rapidly goes gobs the and of flecks of and a chatter sobbings
intersect with which distinct disks of graceful oath,upsoarings the
break on       ceiling-flatness

the Bar.tinking luscious jigs dint of ripe silver with warmlyish
wetflat splurging smells waltz the glush of squirting taps plus slush
of foam knocked off and a faint piddle-of-drops she says I ploc spittle
what the lands thaz me kid in no sir hopping sawdust you kiddo he's a
palping wreaths of badly Yep cigars who jim him why gluey grins topple
together eyes pout gestures stickily point made glints squinting who's
a wink bum-nothing and money fuzzily mouths take big wobbly foot-steps
every goggle cent of it get out ears dribbles soft right old feller
belch the chap hic summore eh chuckles skulch. . . .

and i was sitting in the din thinking drinking the ale,which never
lets you grow old blinking at the low ceiling my being pleasantly was
punctuated by the always retchings of a worthless lamp.

*(CP,* 110)

The second portion of the book, "Chimneys," is made up of sixty-two sonnets divided into three groups, "Sonnets—Realities," "Sonnets—Unrealities," and "Sonnets—Actualities." Although all are, in a stretch of the term, sonnets, the three groups roughly correspond to the three styles we have already identified in earlier chapters. The "Sonnets—Realities" are in the Satyric style. Their subjects are, as we might expect, street markets, tenements, cheap restaurants, pool halls, nightclubs, and other inner-city settings that are peopled with such figures as card players, vagrants (the "twenty seven bums"), belly dancers, prostitutes, and gangsters. Most of the poems of this group are demonstrations that the sonnet form can adapt itself to "unpoetic" subject matter. For example, this one begins like a description from a police blotter:

> "kitty". sixteen,5'1",white,prostitute.
>
> ducking always the touch of must and shall,
> whose slippery body is Death's littlest pal,
>
> skilled in quick softness. Unspontaneous.    cute.
>
> the signal perfume of whose unrepute
> focusses in the sweet slow animal
> bottomless eyes importantly banal,
>
> Kitty. a whore. Sixteen
>                     you corking brute
> amused from time to time by clever drolls
> fearsomely who do keep their sunday flower.
> The babybreasted broad "kitty" twice eight
>
> —beer nothing,the lady'll have a whiskey-sour—
>
> whose least amazing smile is the most great
> common divisor of unequal souls.
>
> (CP, 126)

But in its fresh use of language, the poem goes far beyond the mere ugliness found in the "Portraits" to create both wit and sentiment. For expressing the idea of rules and duties Cummings uses verbs as nouns: "ducking always the touch of must and shall." Kitty's role-playing in order to be cute is conveyed by the words "skilled" and "unspontaneous." A surprise emerges when we encounter "banal" after "bottomless eyes." The metaphorical compactness of "sunday flower" for the virginity of young fellows who teasingly talk with Kitty introduces a tone of scorn for them, especially when it is followed by their own role-playing: the sudden intrusion of their tough talk, "—beer nothing, the lady'll have a whiskey sour—." In fact the shifts of tone in the poem from judgment of Kitty to judgment of the "clever drolls" who joke with her but fear her sexuality are rounded out in a final softening look at Kitty's "least amazing smile" and its power as expressed in mathematical terms. The motifs of "sixteen" and "twice eight" are pulled together in the fact that the number eight is the largest "common divisor" of sixteen.

I should digress to point out that the "Sonnets—Realities," both in the 1922 version of *Tulips & Chimneys* and in *&,* reflect an attitude in which sex is something dirty or repulsive, an attitude telling us that Cummings' upbringing led him to be fearful about sex. Indeed, even though he and Slater Brown became quite friendly with two Parisian prostitutes he kept his "sunday flower" until the night before he left Paris in 1917 to sail home—losing it during a not-entirely-satisfactory experience when he had been taken to bed by a waitress from a couscous restaurant on the rue du faubourg-Montmarte. Thus the speaking voice in the "Sonnets—Realities" is an imagined one, such as "meestaire steevensun" in "when you rang at Dick Mid's Place" (*CP,* 120). As his journals make clear Cummings never visited prostitutes in the United States, nor was he an opportunistic womanizer. On the contrary, he was a virile but rather romantic young man in his treatment of women and was always, in the words of Slater Brown, "a one-woman man."[1] What we can guess then about the grimy subject matter in many of his poems is that it springs from a double origin: his desire to shock The Great American Public as well as his interest in playing off matter against form as one feature of the revolution in literary expression.

The "Sonnets—Unrealities" contain a miscellaneous mixture of poems old and new. There are love poems; considerations of death; observations on the sea, on a garden, on autumn and winter; a tribute to Froissart; cosmic meditations, and so on. The Hephaestian style is sometimes present here but not always under control. There is a lot of apprentice work in these poems as well, some of which are leftovers from Cummings' college years.

The "Sonnets—Actualities," mostly love poems written for Elaine Thayer, are a much more satisfactory mix. The Cummings idiom, with its peculiar jargon of mismatching adjectives such as crisp, skillful, brit-

tle, trite, fragile, precise, exact, and clumsy, is more in evidence than
most readers would wish, but there are also many fresh and startling
images in his descriptions of both city and country scenes and in his tributes to his ladylove. Here, for instance, is one of the monuments he
erects for her:

> my love is building a building
> around you,a frail slippery
> house,a strong fragile house
> (beginning at the singular beginning
>
> of your smile)a skilful uncouth
> prison,a precise clumsy
> prison(building thatandthis into Thus,
> Around the reckless magic of your mouth)
>
> my love is building a magic,a discrete
> tower of magic and(as i guess)
>
> when Farmer Death(whom fairies hate)shall
>
> crumble the mouth-flower fleet
> He'll not my tower,
>             laborious,casual
>
> where the surrounded smile
>         hangs
>
>                   breathless
>                     (*CP*, 165)

On the whole the three groups of sonnets show that Cummings'
judgment was faulty when he made his choices of what to include in his
first book. Either he did not like to discard poems that he had worked
hard to complete, or he could not discriminate his good work from what
was poor. These pages offer plenty of evidence that he would sometimes
allow himself to publish an item of self-conscious pretentiousness just
because he managed to squeeze it into sonnet form. How could he
decide to include this poem from his Rossetti period that begins with
these lines?

O Thou to whom the musical white spring

offers her lily inextinguishable
taught by thy tremulous grace bravely to fling

Implacable death's mysteriously sable
robe from her redolent shoulders . . .

and goes on to apostrophize: "O Love! upon thy dim/ shrine of intangible commemoration . . ." (*CP,* 142). But also to his credit Cummings was a poet who took risks. He often tumbled; yet when he succeeded he achieved that unique quality he strove for.

What is more remarkable is that his judgment was somewhat better than that of his editors. For *XLI Poems,* Lincoln MacVeagh selected most of Cummings' overwrought sonnets that had a "poetic" tone and rejected the more interesting constructs. Thomas Seltzer did better, and the 1923 *Tulips and Chimneys* has enough good material in it to be a valuable contribution to modern poetry. But he too was leery of Cummings' poems that were daunting in their typographical high jinks or that were too openly sexual. As a consequence, for *&* Cummings was left with what he told his typesetter friend, S. A. Jacobs, was his "most personal work."[2] Since *&* was going to be privately published he did not have to worry about censorious editors. Thus he could restore the poems he had withdrawn from the 1919 *Tulips & Chimneys.* This especially affected the sonnets that appeared in the new volume.

Among the "Sonnets—Realities" in *&* were such tough-minded poems as "O It's Nice To Get Up In, the slipshod mucous kiss/ of her riant belly's fooling bore" (*CP,* 203) (which played with allusions to a Harry Lauder song that was popular in the English music halls, "O It's Nice to Get up in the Morning"); "the dirty colors of her kiss have just/ throttled my seeing blood,her heart's chatter/ riveted a weeping skyscraper in me" (*CP,* 205); "the poem her belly marched through me as/ one army" (*CP,* 208); and "her careful distinct sex whose sharp lips comb/ my mumbling grope of strength" (*CP,* 210). These and other "dark lady" sonnets are cleverly composed and filled with exploding metaphors and clashing grammatical elements. One example can stand for the rest:

in making Marjorie god hurried
a boy's body on unsuspicious
legs of girl. his left hand quarried
the quartzlike face. his right slapped
the amusing big vital vicious
vegetable of her mouth.
Upon the whole he suddenly clapped
a tiny sunset of vermouth
-colour.    Hair. he put between
her lips a moist mistake,whose fragrance hurls
me into tears,as the dusty new-
ness of her obsolete gaze begins to.     lean. . . .
a little against me,when for two
dollars i fill her hips with boys and girls

                                                                    (*CP*, 211)

Among the "Sonnets—Actualities" were more that he had created for
Elaine. One outstanding item begins "upon the room's/ silence, i will
sew/ a nagging button of candlelight" (*CP*, 215). The final sonnet in the
group of seven was the finest erotic poem Cummings ever wrote, a
response to the oneness of sexual union that is quiet and delicately direct
in its phrasing.

i like my body when it is with your
body.    It is so quite new a thing.
Muscles better and nerves more.
i like your body.    i like what it does,
i like its hows.    i like to feel the spine
of your body and its bones,and the trembling
-firm-smooth ness and which i will
again and again and again
kiss,    i like kissing this and that of you,
i like,slowly stroking the,shocking fuzz
of your electric fur,and what-is-it comes
over parting flesh....And eyes big love-crumbs,

and possibly i like the thrill

of under me you so quite new

                                                                    (*CP*, 218)

When we look back over this whole collection of poems we can perceive that as a poet Cummings was pulled in three directions. His

unorthodox play with typography, punctuation, and spacing masks this three-way split. Cummings was a lyric poet, ready to sing of love, the moon, the stars, and the beauties of nature, especially flowers. This was the poet who loved the music of Debussy and the painting of Monet. He was also the poet of tough, hard-edged reality, with a leaning toward Juvenalian satire. He liked popular music, the burlesque theater, and the paintings of the "Ash-Can" school. But then too, he was the aesthetic constructionist in poetry who wanted to push language to its outer limits and to introduce visual features into literary expression. He liked the music of Stravinsky, the paintings of Picasso, and the sculpture of Brancusi. As we shall see, these diverse tendencies and tastes persisted throughout his career in varying degrees.

The poems, almost all written before 1920 and published in three separate volumes over the period 1923 through 1925, put Cummings firmly in the center of modern poetry. Even though not all the work he included was worthy of publication there was a solid body of first-rate work here—enough to establish a reputation. As we might expect some critics and reviewers were troubled by or even dismissive of his typographical legerdemain or his Hephaestian distortions, but others grudgingly recorded genuine admiration. Robert L. Wolf, writing in the *New York World,* said, "it is a very disconcerting thing to be compelled to admit, reluctantly, that [*Tulips and Chimneys*] is very good, that it is extraordinarily good, that it contains, in its own individual and unprecedented style, as beautiful poems as have been written by any present-day poet in the English language. When I first read Mr. Cummings' poetry, some years ago in magazines, it inspired me with rage and scorn; from which it appears that disgust is a half-way station on the road to admiration."[3]

Nor did the volumes sell very many copies. It would be another thirteen years before any book of his poems did anything but lose money for publishers and another sixteen years beyond that before his *Poems 1923–1954* brought him unqualified recognition and publishing success.

## Chapter Six

# Jeers, Cheers, and Aspirations

In the midst of his efforts to publish between 1922 and 1925 Cummings faced personal problems of such gravity that they brought about a change in his personality. It all began in 1918 when he fell in love with Elaine Thayer, the wife of his best friend. The Thayer marriage of 1916 had been in trouble for some time, a situation made clear by the fact that the couple now lived in separate apartments on different sides of Washington Square in Greenwich Village. Moreover, Scofield needed to be in Chicago for long periods of time before the *Dial* headquarters moved to New York, and when he traveled he left his wife behind. Out of genuine affection for her, Cummings, Brown, Dos Passos, and other friends frequently spent time with her when her husband was away. Soon a love affair developed between Cummings and the lonely Elaine. Even so he and Scofield remained good friends after Scofield returned to New York permanently. Further complications arose when Elaine became pregnant with Cummings' child and, unwilling to have an abortion, she gave birth to a baby girl in December 1919 while still married to Thayer, who then took on the role of father. Cummings' love affair with Elaine continued intermittently in New York and Paris during the years 1920 to 1924, until the Thayers agreed to divorce in 1921. Cummings finally married Elaine in March 1924 and legally adopted little Nancy who was by then four years old.

But as a self-centered poet and painter Cummings was a very poor husband and father. As a consequence Elaine, neglected once again by Cummings' bachelor-like routine, left him for a wealthy Irish business-man. She officially divorced Cummings in December 1924 and later moved to Ireland, taking Nancy with her and preventing Cummings from having any contact with the child.[1] The loss of both Elaine and Nancy was a psychological blow that depressed Cummings deeply for the next couple of years and left scars for the rest of his life. However unsettling all these troubles were to him, he continued to write and paint in a little studio on the third floor of 4 Patchin Place in the Village. After several months had passed he developed a new love affair with Anne Barton, whom he eventually married in May 1929.

16. PENCIL SKETCHES OF ELAINE
THAYER BY E.E. CUMMINGS.
*Courtesy of the Houghton Library, Harvard
University*

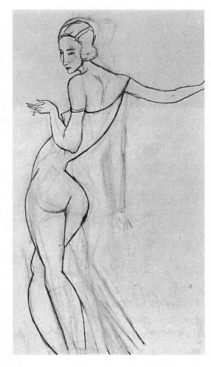

Anne was a former fashion model who had divorced Ralph Barton, a widely published cartoonist known principally for his illustrations in Anita Loos' *Gentlemen Prefer Blondes*. Anne was a good-time woman, lively, witty, and well-suited to the role of the New York flapper of the 1920s. She enjoyed parties with a lot of laughter, drinking, jazz on the phonograph, and dancing. In her vivacity she was very good for Cummings' bruised psyche, but since she was not always faithful to him, she created new problems for him too.

In spite of the disruptions in his personal life during these years, Cummings managed to publish five books and to continue painting and exhibiting at the annual Independent Artists shows. There was a good deal of variety in the books: *Is 5,* a collection of poems (1926); *Him,* an Expressionist play (1927); [No title], a sequence of absurdist narratives (1930); *CIOPW,* a collection of his artwork in charcoal, ink, oil, pencil, and watercolor (1931); and W *(ViVa)* (1931), another book of poems.

*Is 5* reveals some of the strains on Cummings' creativity, for it shows both an advance beyond the *Tulips and Chimneys* poems and a falling off, in that it includes a number of trifles that Cummings should have left in his files. It also includes several poems that had already appeared in the private publication *&,* perhaps an indication that Cummings felt a need to pad—or, more accurately, strengthen—his new volume. There are some new stylistic features however. A few poems are presented in a phonetic rendering of the New York lower-class dialect. For instance, this epigram about a whore and a priest:

now dis "daughter" uv eve(who aint precisely slim)sim

ply don't know duh meanin uv duh woid sin in
not disagreeable contras tuh dat not exacly fat

"father"(adjustin his robe)who now puts on his flat hat
                                                    (*CP,* 238)

Note that the last phrase, describing the priest, is in normal English.

Besides the presence of several linguistic pranks there is occasional evidence that the Dada movement had made an impact on Cummings while he was in Paris in 1921–22. The Dada spirit revels in irrationality of the sort Cummings exhibits in one item that begins in this way:

Will i ever forget that precarious moment?

As i was standing on the third rail waiting for the next train to grind me
into lifeless atoms various absurd thoughts slyly crept into my highly sexed
mind.

It seemed to me that i had first of all really made quite a mistake in being
at all born,seeing that i was wifeless and only half awake,cursed with pimples,
correctly dressed,cleanshaven above the nombril,and much to my astonishment much
impressed by having once noticed(as an infantile phenomenon)George Washington almost incompletely surrounded by well-drawn icecakes beheld being too strong,in
brief:an American,is you understand that i mean what i say i believe my most
intimate friends would never have gathered.

A collarbutton which had always not nothurt me not much and in the same place.

Why according to tomorrow's paper the proletariat will not rise yesterday.

(*CP*, 260)

Of course one principal idea of Dada, which we have encountered
before in Cummings' work, is the necessity to destroy the accepted and
the traditional in order to discover something new and surprising in
artistic effect, or in order to seek some hidden truth that lies beyond the
rational. Hence the title of Cummings' book, which asserts his endeavor
to rise out of the realm where twice two is four.

One distinctive feature of *Is 5* is the presence of a series of antiwar
poems, two of which employ a new satirical device of Cummings', namely the use of allusive quotations or fragments of quotations, a technique
that he learned from T. S. Eliot and Ezra Pound. But unlike Eliot or
Pound he does not employ this technique for general cultural criticism,
rather, he aims to produce real laughter by ridiculing his subjects. In one
of these poems, carefully worked out in sonnet form, he pillories a
Fourth-of-July speechmaker by choosing patriotic and religious clichés
common to platform oratory and compressing fragments of them
together in order to demonstrate by this jumble the meaningless empti-
ness that these appeals have:

> "next to of course god america i
> love you land of the pilgrims' and so forth oh
> say can you see by the dawn's early my
> country 'tis of centuries come and go
> and are no more what of it we should worry
> in every language even deafanddumb
> thy sons acclaim your glorious name by gorry
> by jingo by gee by gosh by gum

why talk of beauty what could be more beautiful than these heroic happy dead
who rushed like lions to the roaring slaughter
they did not stop to think they died instead
then shall the voice of liberty be mute?"

He spoke. And drank rapidly a glass of water

                                              (*CP*, 267)

He goes even further in another of the antiwar poems and uses
repeatedly the Latin phrase "etcetera" to suggest valueless verbiage, until
finally he capitalizes "Etcetera" in order to give it new meaning:

my sweet old etcetera
aunt lucy during the recent

war could and what
is more did tell you just
what everybody was fighting

for,
my sister

isabel created hundreds
(and
hundreds)of socks not to
mention shirts fleaproof earwarmers

etcetera wristers etcetera,my

mother hoped that

i would die etcetera
bravely of course my father used
to become hoarse talking about how it was
a privilege and if only he
could meanwhile my

self etcetera lay quietly
in the deep mud et

cetera
(dreaming,

```
et
    cetera,of
Your smile
eyes knees and of your Etcetera)
```

(*CP*, 275)

In another of the satirical poems he takes fragments of advertising slogans or parodies of brand names of commonly marketed products and mixes them with lines from patriotic songs, this time in an attack on the average American poet. The title is "POEM,OR BEAUTY HURTS MR.VINAL" (Harold Vinal was the editor of *Voices,* a poetry quarterly, and secretary of the Poetry Society of America). It begins with an explosion of phrases:

```
take it from me kiddo
believe me
my country,'tis of

you,land of the Cluett
Shirt Boston Garter and Spearmint
Girl With The Wrigley Eyes(of you
land of the Arrow Ide
and Earl &
Wilson
Collars)of you i
sing:land of Abraham Lincoln and Lydia E. Pinkham,
land above all of Just Add Hot Water And Serve—
from every B.V.D.

let freedom ring . . .
```

(*CP*, 228)

He goes on to a series of scatological jokes while developing his theme that ordinary American poetry is on the same level as advertising copy (or worse, since Cummings calls the poets "throstles," songbirds whose scientific name is "turdus musicus"). The poem ends with a picture of the poets as constipated children straining to produce their poetic results. In the concluding lines the advertised products that he alludes to are Carter's Little Liver Pills, Nujol (a laxative), Kellogg's Bran Flakes ("There's A Reason"), Odorono (an underarm deodorant), and Colgate's Toothpaste.

littleliverpill-
hearted-Nujolneeding-There's-A-Reason
americans(who tensetendoned and with
upward vacant eyes,painfully
perpetually crouched,quivering,upon the
sternly allotted sandpile
—how silently
emit a tiny violetflavoured nuisance:Odor?

ono.
comes out like a ribbon lies flat on the brush

(*CP,* 229)

These three pieces are among the most frequently anthologized of Cummings' poems, even though they are found in this not-very-memorable volume. Another work that is often included in anthologies is the first poem in which Cummings expresses the basic tenet of his Romanticism, the primacy of emotion over reason. It is addressed to a ladylove, and it denigrates anyone who follows rules and systems ("the syntax of things").

since feeling is first
who pays any attention
to the syntax of things
will never wholly kiss you;

wholly to be a fool
while Spring is in the world

my blood approves,
and kisses are a better fate
than wisdom
lady i swear by all flowers.    Don't cry
—the best gesture of my brain is less than
your eyelids' flutter which says

we are for each other:then
laugh,leaning back in my arms
for life's not a paragraph

And death i think is no parenthesis

(*CP,* 291)

17. SELF-PORTRAIT.
INK SKETCH OF
CUMMINGS, 1920S
*Courtesy of the Houghton
Library, Harvard University*

But the assertion about immortality expressed in grammatical terms in the final lines has a subtle qualifier in the phrase "i think." He does not say "i feel."

For all his repeated rejections of thinking and systematic regimentation Cummings took great pains to arrange his collections of poems in orderly patterns. The key number in this book is five. It opens with five sonnets characterizing five prostitutes ("FIVE AMERICANS") and closes with five sonnets addressed to a beloved one. Further, he divides the book into five sections: Part I, linguistic jokes, experiments, and bagatelles; Part II, antiwar poems; Part III, poems set in Europe; Part IV, love poems; Part V, love sonnets. The next volume W (*ViVa*) takes its title from a graffito commonly found on southern European walls, meaning "Long live," as in "Viva Napoli!" or "Viva Presidente Wilson!" Employing a pattern of seven, Cummings arranges seventy poems; every seventh poem is a sonnet, and the last seven poems are all sonnets. The thematic order in *ViVa* is a pattern that he follows in most of his books, starting with *Is 5;* he later described it in a letter to Francis Steegmuller: "to begin dirty (world, sordid, satires) & end clean (earth, lyrical, love poems)."[2]

In spite of the cheeriness of the title the first half of *ViVa* is difficult going. It contains a relentless series of linguistic puzzles with an occasional powerfully expressed satire, such as the first sonnet, which ironically echoes the book's title in its phrase, "LONG LIVE that Upwardlooking/ Serene Illustrious and Beatific/ Lord of Creation, MAN." This poem is a bitter attack on humankind's presumptuousness in an age of new scientific theory, when Space is "curved," life is just a reflex, and "Everything is Relative," with "god being Dead (not to/ mention inTerred)" (*CP,* 317). This is the first of Cummings' attacks on Science, an abstraction that he associates with all that is wrong with the modern world and that he regards as the epitome of unfeeling reason. It is a bugaboo he will chase for the rest of his career.

The thirtieth poem in the collection has become very famous. An antiwar poem that is thematically connected with his hostility toward government and authority, "i sing of Olaf glad and big" is the story of the torture, imprisonment, and death of a conscientious objector during the Great War. Part of its icy irony is brought about by Cummings' having used an irregularly rhymed tetrameter doggerel for such a terrible story. To heighten the irony he chose a formal diction such as one might find in a Victorian moralistic tale about a naughty boy who mistreats the kitten; Cummings occasionally even throws in an archaic word:

> but—though all kinds of officers
> (a yearning nation's blueeyed pride)
> their passive prey did kick and curse
> until for wear their clarion
> voices and boots were much the worse,
> and egged the firstclassprivates on
> his rectum wickedly to tease
> by means of skilfully applied
> bayonets roasted hot with heat—

> Olaf (upon what once were knees)
> does almost ceaselessly repeat
> "there is some shit I will not eat."
>
>                                            (*CP*, 340)

The pose of a medieval balladeer, a François Villon, or a Geoffrey Chaucer, is maintained right up to the end with the summarizing prayer, "Christ (of his mercy infinite)/ i pray to see; and Olaf, too . . ." (*CP*, 340). It is a remarkable production and quite a characteristic subject for "our nonhero, little Estlin."

In the middle of *ViVa* begins a sequence of nature poems, pulled about in the Hephaestian style on such topics as a sunset; an electrical storm; a flower opening its petals; a star at twilight; a moonrise; nature as a transcendent entity; his mother's heaven pictured as a flower garden; a bat at twilight; the dying of life in winter; and a rainfall. The works are in all shapes and jumbles of expression. One of the most fascinating poems is about an electrical storm accompanied by rain, followed by the sun coming out, birds singing, and the refreshment of the earth. The ups and downs of capital and lowercase letters, the pull and push of space, punctuation, and word division make it a dynamic performance.

> n(o)w
>
>           the
> how
>           dis(appeared cleverly)world
>
> iS Slapped:with;liGhtninG
> !
>
>   at
> which(shal)lpounceupcrackw(ill)jumps
>
> of
>    THuNdeRB
>                 loSSo!M iN
> -visiblya mongban(gedfrag-
> ment ssky?wha tm)eani ngl(essNessUn
> rolli)ngl yS troll s(who leO v erd)oma insCol
>
> Lide.!high
>            n , o ;  w   :
>                               theraIncomIng
>
> o all the roofs roar

                        drownInsound(
    &
    (we(are like)dead
                        )Whoshout(Ghost)atOne(voiceless)O
    ther or im)
        pos
        sib(ly as
        leep)
                But l!ook—
                    s


        U
            n:starT birDs(lEAp)Openi ng
    t hing ; s(
    —sing
            )all are aLl(cry alL See)o(ver All)Th(e grEEn

    ?eartH)N,ew

                                                    (*CP*, 348)


Among the love poems one has become especially well known
because it was used by Woody Allen in his film *Hannah and Her Sisters.*
But long before that it was read aloud by many a young man, perhaps
stretched in front of the fireplace on an April night, to his much-adored
girlfriend. It attempts to express the transcendent feeling of response to
the power of a beloved one in the metaphor of the opening and closing
of flower petals. These are the first two of its blank-verse stanzas:

>           somewhere i have never travelled,gladly beyond
>           any experience,your eyes have their silence:
>           in your most frail gesture are things which enclose me,
>           or which i cannot touch because they are too near
>
>           your slightest look easily will unclose me
>           though i have closed myself as fingers,
>           you open always petal by petal myself as Spring opens
>           (touching skilfully,mysteriously)her first rose
>
>                                                   (*CP*, 367)


By 1931 Cummings had become a leading American poet in two
areas—as a satirist and as an experimenter with language in creating
constructs that went beyond what any poetic wordsmith had ever

achieved; in another area he had done commendable work—as a lyric poet, especially in his love poems. But his reputation was limited by two aspects of his career: one, the fault of critics; the other, the fault of himself.

Many critics and reviewers were loathe to acknowledge that the kind of expression Cummings attempted had a high literary value. They regarded him as a trickster and as an iconoclast ready to tear the fabric of literature or undermine the moral basis of society. Yet Cummings himself had helped them to hold their prejudices against his work for he had published a great many poems unworthy of print by a serious poet—much apprentice work appeared in *Tulips and Chimneys* and *XLI Poems* and too many jokes or gimmicky trifles in *Is 5* and *ViVa*. These problems were not going to vanish as time went on. But the very fact that he always had the essential grain in spite of his seeming inability to get rid of chaff meant that a winnowing was possible for anthologists and poetry lovers who could make their own choices. As for the critics and reviewers, they became more used to the Cummings idiom as his books continued to emerge, and what is more, younger judges who were used to reading modern literature were continually arriving on the scene. In time the recognition would come.

## II

Cummings always lived frugally and managed to scrape along by means of occasional prizes, gifts from his father, a small legacy from his grandmother, and what little money his writing brought in. To supplement his income he sometimes wrote comic vignettes under a pseudonym for *Vanity Fair* magazine and illustrated them with line drawings. He had a taste for Dadaesque nonsense, and the editor of *Vanity Fair,* Frank Crowninshield, seemed to tolerate it. Eventually Cummings made a small book of these nonsensical narratives in prose, with each of its nine chapters illustrated by a pen-and-ink sketch. After this series appeared in *New American Caravan* (1929), an annual edited by Alfred Kreymborg and Paul Rosenfeld that was intended to show the work of younger writers, it was published in book form without a title by Covici-Friede in 1930. It was not a significant work. Each chapter weaves a meandering thread of jokes, puns, clichés, burlesques of literary quotations, and narrative nonsequiturs that lead nowhere. It becomes very tiresome reading in a few pages, though some of Cummings' friends seem to have found it entertaining.

## III

A major undertaking in the years following Cummings' problems with marriage, fatherhood, and divorce was his attempt to write a play. Throughout 1926 he had striven to create a dramatic work, going through reams of paper for his notes and drafts, hoping to produce something that was really significant and at the same time "different." At length, after a determined struggle, he completed *Him,* a play that followed the tendencies of Expressionism, a movement in European painting and theater that had its success largely in Scandinavia and Germany.

The Expressionist playwrights professed to show the inner life of the psyche in exterior action, especially in stylized action and stereotypical characters. The first American plays to reflect this mode were Eugene O'Neill's *The Emperor Jones* (1920) and *The Hairy Ape* (1922). But the overearnest Germanic intensity that O'Neill absorbed was not accepted by other American playwrights. Elmer Rice in *The Adding Machine* (1923), John Howard Lawson in *Processional* (1925), and John Dos Passos in *The Garbage Man* (1926)—all had Americanized Expressionism by giving it comic overtones and letting serious ideas emerge through comic distancing.[3]

This American tradition appealed to Cummings, who had discussed literary ideas with both Lawson and Dos Passos. In *Him* he developed a play concerned with the theme of bringing to birth: Me, the heroine, is pregnant; Him, a playwright, is struggling with writer's block while trying to finish his play; and both Him and Me are moving toward a merger as true lovers, not just as an artist and his mistress. In the play Him has many speeches about the creative process and the problems of the artist. Me speaks for another side of Cummings' psyche, and since she frequently states that she has no mind and cannot understand things she represents Cummings' Romantic valuing of feeling over reason. As a character she offers a good counterpoise to the posturing, wisecracking behavior of Him and causes him to mellow into a human being by act 3. These themes, plus other motifs about the unconscious, the problems of identity, and the mysteries of gender are presented in a muddled way by means of the Cummings idiom in dialogue between Him and Me, but also through a series of vaudeville skits, circus sideshows, and carnival barker spiels, which are the liveliest parts of the play.

When the curtain rises we see a hospital scene, with Me being anesthetized on an operating table. (Cummings is here consciously alluding to the opening lines of T. S. Eliot's "The Love Song of J. Alfred Prufrock.") Besides the doctor, onstage are the three Weird Sisters, the Fates, who in Greek mythology preside over childbearing and the destinies of human beings. They sit in rocking chairs, knitting the threads of destiny, and chatting in a mixture of twisted proverbs, advertising slogans, and trite phrases of neighborly gossip. This scene recurs five times in the play, although the number nine, which stands for the period of gestation, is the key figure in the pattern of the play.[4]

The next scene is the "Room" where Him and Me conduct their dialogue. Me is complaining about Him's neglect of her and hints to the audience of her pregnancy. Him, preoccupied with his play, responds absently or spouts joking nonsense, although at one point he talks about the creative achievement of the artist in a frequently quoted metaphor involving the circus acrobat:

> imagine a human being who balances three chairs, one on top of another, on a wire, eighty feet in air with no net underneath, and then climbs into the top chair, sits down, and begins to swing. . . . it is such a perfect acrobat! The three chairs are three facts—it will quickly kick them out from under itself and will stand on air. . . . it rocks carefully and smilingly on three facts, on: I am an Artist, I am a Man, I am a Failure—it rocks and it swings and it smiles and it does not collapse tumble or die because it pays no attention to anything except itself. (12–13)

When Me asks to see parts of the play he is writing Him agrees, and we are offered nine vaudeville skits,[5] most of which have comic reference to psychological problems or processes. For example, in one scene a man carrying a trunk marked "fragile" is stopped by a policeman. The man says that the trunk is his unconscious, although he does not know what is in it. When the policeman finally opens it and peers in he collapses in a dead faint. Some of the scenes were at that time recognizable parodies of elements in recent Broadway plays or musical comedies. One, in which two men named Bill and Will wear masks and engage in a "Who's-on-first?"-kind of dialogue, pokes fun at O'Neill's *The Great God Brown*. Another, in which two men meet six times, exchange cryptic greetings, and then pop balloons with their cigars, is a parody of a Broadway musical number, "How's tricks?" Another scene, set in ancient Rome and presenting four fluttering homosexuals in togas, is Cummings' burlesque of the comic sketches frequently found in burlesque theaters—thus, a burlesque of burlesque.

The most elaborate of the scenes has a Negro ensemble singing a bawdy version of "Frankie and Johnie."[6] (When *Him* was published in 1927 Cummings had a battle with Liveright, his publisher, over his right to include the line about Johnie "finger-fucking Nellie Bly"—a battle that he lost.) Toward the end of the song a censorious figure, John Rutter, the president of the Society for the Contraception of Vice (a jibe at John S. Sumner, head of the New York Society for the Suppression of Vice), arises from the audience and objects to the song just as the singers are about to utter a vernacular word for penis. But he is frightened away when Frankie advances down nine stairs and presents him with an amputated penis in a bloody napkin, "the best part of the man who done me wrong" (56).

After more meandering dialogue between Him and Me and another burlesque sketch, this time set in Paris (Him's dream, in which he appears carrying a head of cabbage and declaring "I was born the day before yesterday"), the play reaches its climax as Me hears a drumbeat suggesting the heartbeat of her child, and the scene merges into a circus sideshow, presumably the bizarre contents of Me's unconscious, in which a barker presents eight circus performers: the nine-foot giant, the tattooed man, the six hundred pounds of passionate pulchritude, and so on. The ninth attraction is the dancer, Princess Anankay (Greek for Necessity), announced as "the undiluted original milkshake of the ages . . . the world's first and foremost exponent of the yaki-hula-hiki-dula otherwise known as the Royal Umbilical Bengal Cakewalk" (I have translated the barker's dialect). But when the curtains open Me stands holding a newborn baby. Him utters "a cry of terror" and the three Weird Sisters exclaim, "It's all done with mirrors!" (144).

The play ends with a brief scene in which Him and Me are back in the Room once more, as if the previous scene had never taken place. Me, facing the footlights, points out to Him that the audience represents the real world; the actors and the play are only what the audience pretends is real.

Although Cummings' notes and drafts show that he was working with a fascinating complex of ideas,[7] he was not actually able to bring them alive in dramatic form in this play. An uncut version of *Him* runs almost four hours,[8] a wearisome evening given the obscurities of Cummings' dialogue and the lack of clarity between parts. The most disappointing feature, however, is the conclusion. In the last scene there is no reference to the baby, to the relationship between Him and Me, or to

Him's play. The turn to the audience is merely a mechanical device in the guise of a statement on imagination and reality.

Since its publication *Him* has been produced from time to time by little theater groups. Its initial production, in a cut version, at the Provincetown Playhouse in Greenwich Village in 1928 was its most successful, for it had a full professional cast and production staff.[9] The play ran for twenty-seven performances to full houses of 200 people in the small theater at 133 MacDougal Street. It appealed to the Playhouse clientele—intellectuals, bohemians, and academics—who could appreciate the allusions to literature and psychoanalysis and delighted in the combination of learned wit and carnival-show atmosphere in the vaudeville skits. No one was quite sure what the play was about, and a controversy about its value arose that was carried on between the Broadway reviewers and Cummings' friends and supporters, who published a pamphlet edited by Gilbert Seldes entitled *him and the critics*.[10] What seems clear is that the play became a kind of Rorschach blot enacted on stage; thus the members of the audience were really responding to the preperformance "Warning" that Cummings printed in the program: "Relax and give the play a chance to strut its stuff—relax, stop wondering what it's all 'about,'—like many strange things, Life included, this Play isn't 'about,' it simply is. . . . Don't try to enjoy it, let it try to enjoy you. DON'T TRY TO UNDERSTAND IT, LET IT TRY TO UNDERSTAND YOU."[11]

As time went on Cummings tried his hand at drama now and again, but except for a short Christmas play, *Santa Claus,* which we will take note of later, he never succeeded in getting any farther than notes and schemes.

## Chapter Seven
# A Trip Through Hell? No Thanks

By 1930 Cummings had traveled widely in western Europe—France, Italy, Portugal, Spain, Germany—but like other of his literary contemporaries he was curious about Russia and the conflicting reports he had heard about the success or failure of the great social experiment of the twentieth century. His friend, the biographer M. R. Werner, had a grim report of his experience there, whereas John Dos Passos was enthusiastic about what he had seen, especially the new work in the theater. Equally confusing views came from French and Russian friends in Paris. Thus Cummings decided to travel there and find out for himself, although, devotee of individualism that he was, he did not expect to be overwhelmed by the joys of collectivism.

After some difficulty he was able to secure a special "without party" visa so that he could avoid being herded about with a group of tourists seeing Potemkin villages. He left from Paris on May 10, 1931, for a five-week trip that took him to Moscow, Kiev, and Odessa, then to Istanbul, returning by the Orient Express to Paris on June 14.[1] What he discovered was more depressing than what Werner had warned him about. The celebrator of the Verb "Is" found a "World of Was," run by bureaucrats who specialized in inefficiency, indifference, delay, and "nyet." Moscow struck him as a place where everything was rickety, shoddy, ramshackle, out-of-date, and dilapidated. Although Cummings himself was not an overly fastidious person he was surprised by the filth, ugliness, "everywhere dirt and cracked fingernails,"[2] and was repulsed by the stink of crowding human bodies, of garbage, rot, and mildew, of unsanitary cafés and toilet facilities. The zombie-like demeanor of the Moskovites made him feel that "verily, verily have I entered a new realm whose inhabitants are made of each other" (21). As he says in *Eimi,* "nobody seems anything but lonesome; hideously lonesome in hideousness, in rundownness, in outattheheelsness, in neglectedness, in strictly omnipotent whichandwhatness" (10). Because of their dispiritedness, they were often given to "That Elsewhere Look" (32).

Although the Intourist Agency had at first isolated him in the Hotel Metropole, a luxury hotel reserved for foreigners, he ran into an acquaintance from Cambridge, Henry Wadsworth Longfellow Dana, who was studying the Russian theater and who became a guide to many representative parts of the city. Cummings was thus able to absorb the atmosphere of Moscow through his rather ordinary activities: going to the bank, trying to get permission to travel to Odessa, trying to change his living quarters, delivering gifts to Lili Brik[3] (whom he called Madame Potiphar in *Eimi*) from her sister in Paris, meeting Russian writers and American newspapermen, going to the theater, the opera, the circus, the art museum, and visiting Lenin's Tomb.

On his first visit to the theater he discerned the heavy hand of the state upon art: "a pondiferously (and How) YMCA atmosphere . . . everywhere a mysterious sense of behaving, of housebrokenness, of watch-your-stepism" (32). Even though he met many defenders of the Soviet system he observed a widespread fear of the secret police, the GPU. Eventually toward the end of his visit he himself felt the fear and even an apprehension about whether or not he would be able to get out of the country. Fortunately he was adopted by an American couple, Mr. and Mrs. Charles Malamuth, who invited him to share their apartment in a former mansion for the last part of his Moscow stay. Malamuth, a foreign correspondent, and his charming wife Joan (Jack London's daughter) not only arranged for him to meet many Russian writers and members of the American colony, but they also provided a sound perspective on Russian culture and the Soviet system, for Malamuth had been originally attracted by the socialist experiment but later came to see what had gone wrong.

When Cummings traveled to Kiev however he gained a sense of "the Old Russia" (265). Here were trees, rivers, churches. He observed the evening walk-around of the young people and rejoiced in seeing them dancing. On the trains to Kiev and Odessa, traveling second and third class, he came into contact with many ordinary Russians with whom he had good rapport despite problems with the language. But here he had two close encounters with the GPU, whose officials arrogantly questioned the passengers and examined their baggage. In Odessa he acquired another mentor who showed him the sights, including the mud beach and its grotesquely daubed patrons. He called upon the mother of his Berlitz Russian teacher and delivered a few simple gifts. From Odessa he sailed across the Black Sea to Istanbul, where he visited St. Sophia and the Blue Mosque twice before his three-day train journey back to Paris.

During his travels he secretly kept a diary that later formed the basis for his book *Eimi,* which in Greek means "I am."

## II

According to Charles Norman, his first biographer, Cummings made no additions to or changes in his diary when he brought it out as *Eimi,* an account of his Russian travels.[4] But Norman must have misunderstood what Cummings was telling him, for *Eimi* is about ten times the length of the diary. Cummings expanded his cryptic entries fully, supplied extensive dialogue for the many characters who people its pages, added a number of personal meditations on his experience, and gave a characteristic visual or linguistic arrangement to many passages. The result was as consciously crafted a literary text as Thoreau's *Walden.*

*Eimi* is Cummings' most important prose work, but it is also his least accessible to the general reader. In 1933 many reviewers of the first edition denounced it as impenetrable: some declared they could not read it; others openly admitted that they did not finish it. Because of these complaints Cummings supplied a "Sketch for a Preface" for a later edition in 1958, in which he clarified for the reader the principal characters and their nicknames and included a day-by-day summary of his activities to guide the reader's understanding of the sequence of events in the narrative. He also added a translated list of the Russian words that he had used in the text.[5] These efforts have encouraged many more readers to attempt the rewarding task of reading this much-neglected masterwork.

As in *The Enormous Room* Cummings provided a mythic framework for his narrative, and this time it was The Journey to the Underworld (or the Unworld, as he calls Soviet Russia). The principal myth was Dante's *La Divina Comedia.* The time spent in Russia corresponds to the *Inferno,* in which Dante, "in the midst of the journey of life," has wandered from the true path and, in order to reach a heavenly goal, is granted gracious help by his beloved, Beatrice, and is guided through the levels of Hell by Virgil until he descends to its ultimate depth where he finds Satan himself, the essence of evil. Leaving Hell Dante passes through Purgatory and finally reaches Paradise where he achieves a mystical vision of God. Although Cummings does not follow the exact allegorical details as he goes along, there are a number of correspondences that give extra dimension to his narrative. He was thirty-six years old at the time of his journey through Russia. Dana, his first guide in Moscow, is called Virgil (and sometimes Sibyl, the prophet who guided Aeneas in his journey to the underworld). The gracious Joan Malamuth represents Beatrice. The visit to Lenin's Tomb is the Vision of Satan. The time spent in Istanbul is

18. PENCIL SKETCH OF NOTRE DAME DE PARIS, 1922, BY E. E. CUMMINGS.
*Courtesy of the Houghton Library, Harvard University*

Purgatory, and France, is Paradise, where at the end of the book, Cummings has a mystical identification with the Spirit of Creativity.

Some of the difficulties that readers confront in *Eimi* are merely aspects of the Cummings idiom that he employed in writing sonnets or that he used in letters to his friends. This style is easy enough to get used to, although when Cummings introduces common words and phrases in French, German, Italian, Latin, and even Russian, readers unacquainted with these languages are unable to understand some passages (one wonders especially what readers of the early edition were able to make of the Russian words that were phoneticized into English pronunciation). Cummings also "masked" the characters, as he said in the preface, so they could not be identified by the Russian authorities, but this also makes for difficult reading since he keeps changing the nicknames that he gives them. Dana is referred to as Virgil, Sibyl, mentor, ex-mentor, ex-, childface, and so on. Charles Malamuth is Turk, the Assyrian, and That Bourgeois Face; Joan is Turkess, Harem, Beatrice. Almost everyone gets abbreviated nicknames. The "1/2 bald hotel clerk" is soon "hb." A character named Pickwick has a private secretary who becomes "p.s." and later the two are "P" and "p." Cummings himself appears as Comrade Kem-min-kz (the way the Russians pronounce his name); Comrade K; K; Peesahtel (writer); Hoodozhnik (painter); and Poietes (Greek for "poet").

A further problem is posed by Cummings' practice of jumping abruptly, without explanation or transition (except for a space in the text), into a new scene, which is often unidentifiable without referring back to the preface for guidance—and sometimes not even then. Moreover without warning Cummings will insert flashbacks that can be a complete mystery to the reader unfamiliar with Cummings' life. For example, on the train to Russia he is being shown picture postcards by a traveling companion when suddenly this passage intrudes: "seated on the terrace of the maggots,announce "je vais faire un petit voyage en Russie" . . . Larionov rolls back-and-sideways—"Voo?" . . . "Moi" . . . His eyes tighten;quizzically his big face lunges:spinning pours tumbling sounds at Gontcharova,who starts; stares—"Vous?" . . . "Moi" . . . Pain heaps quickly itself up in her eyes;caving (memory) surges outward as wish . . . relaxing, her life how very much more than quietly affirms, You are right:Spring is nowhere else" (11). Cummings had reverted to a memory of sitting in front of the restaurant Les Deux Magots in Paris, telling his friend, the painter Michael Larionov, of his planned trip to Russia. After Larionov tells this in Russian to his wife, the painter Natalie Gontcharova, she reacts, remembering her homeland and the beautiful springtime there. But the reader without knowledge of Cummings' life will have a problem understanding all this.[5] A fully annotated edition of *Eimi* would be about double the length of the book itself.

The troubles in reading *Eimi* should not be overstressed, however, for the experience is similar to lingering over some of the difficult chapters in Joyce's *Ulysses* where in spite of problem passages, and indeed with the added intellectual invigoration of coping with allusions and linguistic acrobatics, the reader experiences a deep enjoyment. A good part of the pleasure in *Eimi* lies in the display of Cummings' comic genius. Since the book is both comic and satiric, it ranges through farce, burlesque, parody, mimicry, invective, wit, and several kinds of irony. Cummings' ability at mimicry allows him to provide very suitable dialogue for his characters, for example, the old-maidish fussiness and gossipiness of Dana or the juvenile slang of a young American college boy in Istanbul. His descriptions can have a comic aptness. An ancient Russian taxi is "a fiacre crossed with a catastrophe"; the driver is "a looney Santa Claus, whose 8 tiny reindeer consist of something very (very) distantly resembling a horse" (14); a dining car on a bumpy train is "this Ritz on square wheels" (10). In another wryly comic passage he is supposed to be met at the Moscow train station by Lidin, a Russian poet, and wonders how he will be recognized, speculating that possibly in Russia writers are supposed to know each other: "However,dogs will be dogs and Pavlov,with the aid of lampposts,may have discovered a brand-new recognition reflex" (13).

He twists a great many allusions or common sayings into forms that have a Russian or Marxist reference: "Marx helps those who help themselves" (364); "argue until the comrade cows come home"; "this little bit of Eaven on Hearth, Marxland" (92); "looking as if he had been hit by a batch of 5 year plans and several collective farms to boot" (331); and arguments that the new economics "make sun while the hay shines, opens the key of life with the lock of science, . . . and justifies from soup to nuts the ways of Marx to man" (83).

There is a stylistic richness here that bears more likeness to his poetry than to the prose of *The Enormous Room*. In *Eimi* Cummings plays with language in ways both old and new: 1) by distorting popular sayings and well-known quotations, as described above; 2) by using puns, spoonerisms, portmanteau words, and witty combinations of any sort (between the "T. S. Waistline and the Eliot," 36); 3) by violating common grammatical usage (using adjectives and adverbs as nouns, nouns as verbs, and so on); 4) by jumbling the accepted syntactical order within sentences; 5) by intertwining words (a drunk falls "sudflopdenpingly in nearest gutter," 77); 6) by substituting an allusive reference for a direct reference (barbed wire is "worldwarwire," 153); 7) by throwing into the text common words and phrases from foreign languages ("Sie could have felled ich. With a moonbeam," 277); 8) by using phonetically spelled dialects of English; 9) by mixing slang or colloquial phrasing with learned or archaic terms; 10) by juggling punctuation marks and capital letters for special effects; 11) and by using any and all devices of verse: rhyme, alliteration, spacing, metaphor, and so on. The intermingling of all these ways of manipulating words produces somewhat of a linguistic cabaret performance, the end result of which is comic poetry.

But most of the satirical criticism is serious. Cummings conveys the essential qualities of the Russian Unworld by means of a series of linguistic negatives. Comrade Kem-min-kz visits the "cityless city" of Moscow, changes his traveler's checks at a "bankless bank," and receives

"moneyless money" (roubles). At a restaurant he is served "nonmeat."
The Russian women are so lacking in femininity that they can only be
called "nonmales"; Cummings' pronoun reference for them is "unhe."
Windows always seem to be shut, keeping out fresh air ("aria fresca"), so
that he refers to them as a "shutness," or later, simply as a "shut" (3).
Indeed "SHUT" is the opening word in the book and becomes a literary
motif as the narrative goes on—to be countered by the final word of the
book, which is "OPENS."

Soviet Russia as pictured in *Eimi* seems the complete negation of
Cummings' philosophy of "Is," that human beings should live so as to
express their own individuality—to be "alive"; to place a value on feeling, on growing, on diversity, on "being continually born"; to pursue
happiness; to cherish freedom; to rejoice in pleasure; to give and respond
to love. Cummings felt that the Soviet system was stifling the life out of
its people. Everywhere in Moscow he sensed "nonlife" or mere
"undeath." He found fear, guilt, and a dispirited sameness; a "whichness
and whatness" instead of a "whoness"; a lack of laughter; a suspicion of
pleasure ("in Russia, everybody's leisure is organized," 146); and emphasis on forced behavior. A key passage is an analogy to the life process of a
caterpillar/butterfly:

> did you ever keep caterpillars did you ever have them make cocoons
> did you ever wait did you ever hear a rustling a dim thudding a des-
> perate thin knocking it was a moth trying to escape from the
> cocoon but something is wrong it can't it will die in there you must
> help it you really can't help helping it you can't stand the tinying
> noise you slit the cocoon Out Flops A Monstrous Unthing which
> Dies dies because it did Not escape Itself because it was Helped
> because it canNot Grow you let it out but It Cannot Grow it had
> better died inside the Cocoon at least that would have been a natur-
> al death a doom caused by itself's weakness by itself's inability to
> burst forth and to live! living to grow! growing to be. (323)

His own basic view of life pushed Cummings toward sympathy with
something that Russia had suppressed—religion, which he associated
with that whole side of life he revered—feeling, spirit, innerness, and all
qualities that cannot be measured. This sympathetic tendency emerges
in repeated contrasts between the baroque glories of St. Basil's, the
church that he refers to as "Arabian Nights" or "Something Fabulous"
(25), and the bleak structure of Lenin's Mausoleum. The depth that
Comrade Kem-min-kz descends to in the visit to Lenin's Tomb has its

counterbalance toward the end of the book when Cummings' "heroless hero" enters St. Sophia in Istanbul, where the vastness of the interior inspires a perception of himself, a "dark poet; blindman," as "darkly communing with impossible light." The passage is full of paradoxical language, but it connects with the conclusion of the book, as Cummings appears to recognize the spirit of creativity within himself:

> . . . his
>         voice is made of silence and when his voice pauses the
>     silence is made of voice.
>         (Silently
>                 as now to
>                         whom my,pray-
>                                     ing my
>         self;bows)

                                                                (406)

On the train trip back to Paris another meditation occurs that hurls defiance against mechanism. While the train is stopped at a station Cummings addresses the locomotive, the "metal steed," the false "wheel-god," the mere "go-toy," and contrasts it with the Spirit he feels within himself, "Whose will is to dream and Whose language is silence" (418), words that personify the unconscious self that is also the power beneath creativity in all human beings.

These two passages prepare the reader for the concluding lines of *Eimi,* which are otherwise puzzling, almost incoherent. Cummings is attempting to express something similar to an Emersonian transcendental experience, a mystical union with the creative force. In the final passage the speaker identifies himself first with the advance of the seasons toward winter and snow (starrise and moonrise are also taking place), and then with the "Voice of silence" itself:

> leaning I am this hurling inexhaustibly from june huge rushing
>     upon august until whirlingly with
>     harvest huger happens bloodily prodigious october
>
> . . . . . . . . . . . . . . . . . . . . . . . . . . . . . .
>     finally
>     (and what
>     stars)descendingly assuming
>     only shutting gradually this
>     perfection(and I am)becoming

> silently
>             made
>                     of
>                             silent.
>                                         &
>
> silence is made of
>             (behind perfectly or
>             final rising
>             humbly
>             more dark
>             most luminous proudly
>             whereless fragrant whenlessly erect
>             a sudden the!entirely blossoming)
>
> Voice
>             (Who:
>             Loves;
>             Creates,
>             Imagines)
>             OPENS

                                                              (431–32)

Cummings had been brought up in the Unitarian Church, which, though greatly secularized at the time, recognized that its roots and early development ran parallel to New England Transcendentalism. It seems that the trip to Russia had pushed Cummings back to his New England heritage.

Although the book is too long, given the difficulties of its style *Eimi* is an outstanding achievement. Cummings called it a novel, but even that all-embracing term for literary narrative seems inaccurate. In another discussion I have put it in the category of prose narrative that I call fictional thesaurus, a genre I define as a long literary narrative made up of shorter units in prose or verse in which the parts are joined together by chronology or association of ideas rather than by probable and necessary development.[7] This genre displays a mixture of styles and variations in mood but, taken together, presents a coherent thematic statement or view on life. It achieves some unity through the actions of a single character or the voice of a single narrator. I have in mind such works as Irving's *Knickerbocker's History of New York,* De Quincy's *Confessions of an English Opium Eater,* Wolfe's *Of Time and the River,* Dos Passos' *U.S.A.,*

Huxley's *Ape and Essence,* and Toomer's *Cane.* In these works, the very fact that they have a mixture of material places an emphasis on part rather than whole, giving them an anthology-like quality. Readers have a habit of revisiting them for the reading of chosen parts. *Eimi* is a book that can be read once studiously but can be later picked up and browsed through as with a collection of poems.

# III

The poems gathered in Cummings' next book of poems, *No Thanks* (1935), correspond in spirit to *Eimi* in their fierceness of rejection and in their final affirmation that has religious or transcendental overtones. The two books are also similar in that they reach the apex of linguistic play: there are more successful experiments with technique in *No Thanks* than in any previous or subsequent volume of Cummings' creations. Although this book's publication met with a disdain that equalled the bleak reception of *Eimi,* Cummings had taken great pains to arrange its material in a careful pattern. After playing around with the order of the poems for some time he finally arrived at a "schema" (he took the word from Dante's patterns for *La Divina Comedia*) wherein he began the book with two moon poems and ended it with two star poems. But between these extremities he conceived of a descent downward from the height of the moon to the earth-darkness at the middle of the seventy-one poems in a way that a mystic descends to the dark night of the soul. This is the poem at the nadir:

> into a truly
> curving form
> enters my
> soul
>
> feels all small
> facts dissolved
> by the lewd guess
> of fabulous immensity
>
> the sky screamed
> the sun died)
> the ship lifts
> on seas of iron

breathing height eating
steepness the
ship climbs
murmuring silver mountains

which
disappear(and
only
was night

and through only this night a
mightily form moves
whose passenger and whose
pilot my spirit is

                                        (*CP,* 419)

This little myth is not only an assertion of the formidable presence of the poet's essential being (note the final word, "is"), but it is also an allegory of creation, in which the soul of the poet enters into the form, feels facts dissolve, passes though crises, and emerges as the force in command of the form, which is in movement developing meaning.

On each side of this centrally located poem is a sonnet. The first (poem 35) reaches down in the darkness to depict the earth being overwhelmed by an incoming tide, and it concludes:

meanwhile this ghost goes under,his drowned girth
are mountains;and beyond all hurt of praise
the unimaginable night not known

                                        (*CP,* 418)

The other sonnet (poem 37) moves out of the darkness to call for the creation of a man, a heroic life-bringer who will give away more than he may have. It concludes:

"—open your thighs to fate and (if you can withholding
nothing)World,conceive a man"

                                        (*CP,* 420)

Along the way down from moon height to this depth of night and along the way up again to star height are ranged poems in sequences of three followed by a sonnet. Cummings sketched out the overall design in his notes thus:

FINAL SCHEMA

°2 moons        •2 stars

('mOOn Over tOwns mOOn')        ('brIght')

('moon over gai')     ('morsel   miraculous   and    meaningless')

NO THANKS:schema of construction

| °2 poems | 2 poems• |
|---|---|
| sonnet I | sonnet XVIII |
| 3 poems | 3 poems |
| sonnet II | sonnet XVII |
| 3 poems | 3 poems |
| sonnet III | sonnet XVI |
| 3 poems | 3 poems |
| sonnet IV | sonnet XV |
| 3 poems | 3 poems |
| sonnet V | sonnet XIV |
| 3 poems | 3 poems |
| sonnet VI | sonnet XIII |
| 3 poems | 3 poems |
| sonnet VII | sonnet XII |
| 3 poems | 3 poems |
| sonnet VIII | sonnet XI |
| 3 poems | 3 poems |

('how dark and single,where—sonnet IX      sonnet X—('conceive a man,should he

he ends,the earth')       I poem           have anything')[8]

('into a truly')

As for the poems themselves, *No Thanks* contains a virtuosity in conveying ideas by means of visual arrangements, something that Cummings never attempted again: it is thus the most technically interesting book of poems that he ever published. He intertwines words and phrases; repeats words, syllables, letters, or punctuation marks for special meaning; runs some words together and breaks others into pieces; forces words to function in ways they never did before; and creates his own grammar in putting his sentences together. What is most satisfying is that, while employing these methods, he manages to compose so many aesthetically successful works, whereas in *Is 5* and *ViVa* so much of the wordplay was mere exercise.

At the end of one poem about a foggy dawn that is gradually penetrated by the sun there is a disclosure of the objects in the natural scene likened to the creation of the universe, as the sun coming through the mistiness "mmamakmakemakesWwOwoRworLworlD" (*CP,* 423). In another piece spring is celebrated as the hurdy-gurdy man appears play-

19. E. E. CUMMINGS AT
PATCHIN PLACE, NEW
YORK CITY, 1937
*Courtesy of the Houghton
Library, Harvard University*

ing his instrument, which is slightly out of tune. The words of the poem
say "or a sour hand organ bleats sweet nothings or a rancid hurdy gurdy
gurgling thumps something (while sparrows wince," but in order to convey the off-key sounds, the words are broken up in this way: "!o-ras-ourh
an-dorg-an ble-at-ssw-ee-t-noth ings orarancidhurd/ ygurdygur glingth
umpssomet hings(whi,le sp,arrow,s wince" (*CP,* 442).

A poem describing the sound of snow falling and eventually suggesting the presence of a frost god cannot be read aloud. For its effect it
must be *seen* on the page, yet it is presenting *sound.*

emptied.hills.listen.
,not,alive,trees,dream(
ev:ery:wheres:ex:tend:ing:hush

)
andDark
IshbusY
ing-roundly-dis

tinct;chuck
lings,laced

ar:e.by(

fleet&panelike&frailties
!throughwhich!brittlest!whitewhom!
f
  l o a t ?)
     r
      h y t h m s

                                                *(CP,* 416)

In another poem the action of an ant is set down in broken and intertwined words and phrases as Cummings plays with the Biblical quota-
tion, "Go to the ant thou sluggard; consider her ways and be wise." The
poem begins:

go(perpe)go

(tu)to(al
adve

nturin
g p
article

s of s
ini
sterd
exte

ri)go to(ty)the(om
nivorou salways lugbrin
g ingseekfindlosin g
motilities
are)go to

the
ant
(al
ways

alingwaysing) . . .

                                                *(CP,* 403)

A striptease performer in another sketch shows the suspense of hesi-
tation and delay as she begins

```
unununun?
butbutbut??
tonton???
ing????
```

(CP, 444)

One especially brilliant item is the penultimate star poem, "brIght." As Robert McIlvaine has pointed out, there are only eleven discrete words used in the fifteen-line poem, but they are handled in such a way that they make up a total of forty-four words: the three-letter words "big," "yes," and "who" occur three times; the four-letter words "soft," "near," "calm," "holy," "deep," and "star," four times; the five-letter word "alone," five times; the six-letter word "bright," six times.[9] As the poem develops, the religious overtones build:

```
brIght

bRight s??? big
(soft)

soft near calm
(Bright)
calm st?? holy

(soft briGht deep)
yeS near sta? calm star big yEs
alone
(wHo

Yes
near deep whO big alone soft near
deep calm deep
????Ht ?????T)
Who(holy alone)holy(alone holy)alone
```

(CP, 455)

In the poem the "star" comes into being as the question marks are removed, while the word "bright" disappears. Meanwhile the capital letters accumulate to spell out BRIGHT, YES, and WHO as if the disappearing "bright" has merged into the "yes" and the "who," terms that reverberate with associations suggesting affirmation and a transcendent being. At the same time the length of the stanzas (line groups) has

20. PENCIL SKETCHES OF STRIPTEASE
DANCERS BY E. E. CUMMINGS.
*Courtesy of the Houghton Library, Harvard
University*

increased as the poem moves toward the final line, whose repetitions
echo the phrase "wholly alone." The repetition of "calm," "holy," and
"bright" suggest the poem is about the Star of Bethlehem because of
their allusion to the Christmas hymn "Silent night, holy night/ All is
calm, all is bright."

What Cummings had in mind here, whether consciously or not, is his
father's preaching "the Religion of the Star," for Edward Cummings was
dissatisfied with the Christian symbol of the cross. As a Unitarian he pre-
ferred the symbol of the star and the joyous spirit of "good will to men"
that the angels sang over the Bethlehem stable. In any case this linguistic construct, which is not even a syntactical unit—this "fait," as
Cummings once wanted to call a modernist poem—is one of his prime
achievements in the manipulation of language and typography.

In ways like these the poems present a great variety of scenes and
experiences. There are two poems about boxing matches, each creating the effect of exchanges of blows, with one ending in a knock-
out. Another poem pays homage to the tap dancer Paul Draper,
suggesting his movement visually. A sonnet gives us the blur of a
European city's streets as a horse pulls a wagon full of flowers
("what a proud dreamhorse"). In another poem we hear, phonetically rendered, one end of a frequently interrupted telephone conversation ("o"). In still another birds dart through the air at twilight
("birds("). And another poem allows us to see/hear church bells on a
bright Sunday morning ("(b").

There is some light verse in *No Thanks* too. A good example is the
epigram on Ernest Hemingway.

> what does little Ernest croon
> in his death at afternoon?
> (kow dow r 2 bul retornis
> wus de woids uf lil Oinis
>
> (*CP,* 409)

Many readers have puzzled over these lines because of Cummings'
allusions and his phonetic spelling of New York dialect. The opening line
is a parody of Tennyson's "Cradle Song," found in his poem "Sea
Dreams": "What does little birdie say/ In her nest at peep of day?" But
a stanza from Longfellow's poem "The Psalm of Life" hovers more mali-
ciously over the epigram:

> Life is real! Life is earnest!
> And the grave is not the goal;
> Dust thou art, to dust returnest
> Was not spoken of the soul.

Although Cummings admired Hemingway's early work, he did not care for the macho pose of the 1930s, and he enjoyed reading Max Eastman's review of *Death in the Afternoon,* entitled "Bull in the Afternoon."[10] Thus came into being Cummings' cradle song for Hemingway, hinting at infantile views, a lack of manliness (cow thou art), and a propensity for bull-slinging (to bull returnest).

There are several poems in the volume devoted to love and its mysteries, especially as the book draws to its close in its climb toward the stars. But the title *No Thanks* is a negative one, an attitude for which Cummings had justification. He had published nine books and exhibited his paintings frequently, yet his work was still not recognized adequately. He dedicated *No Thanks* to the fourteen publishers who rejected his manuscript, their names arranged on the dedication page in the shape of a funeral urn. The literary world had changed for him, partly because of the economic depression of the 1930s. The *Dial* had ceased publication; many of his friends had left town. He felt isolated from other literary contemporaries, mostly leftists who shunned him because of his strong anticommunist views. In addition he had suffered another serious psychological blow. In 1932 his wife Anne, whose instability as a mate had caused him much anguish, ran off with a surgeon, Dr. Joseph Girdansky.

Thematically there is a great deal of darkness in *No Thanks.* Cummings' individualism had expanded into increasingly negative attitudes toward American culture: there is not only the usual ridicule of politicians and businessmen but also satire directed against the rituals of baseball ("o pr"); the Chicago World's Fair—A Century of Progress— ("out of a supermetamathical subpreincestures"); the pretentions of iconoclastic literary magazines ("let's start a magazine/ to hell with literature/ we want something redblooded"); and against "most (people." His former scorn for the taste of The Great American Public has become an attack on its whole existence personified:

> he does not have to feel because he thinks
> (the thoughts of others,be it understood)
> he does not have to think because he knows
> (that anything is bad which you think good)

21. PENCIL SKETCHES OF ANNE
BARTON BY E. E. CUMMINGS.
*Courtesy of the Houghton Library, Harvard
University*

because he knows,he cannot understand
(why Jones don't pay me what he knows he owes)
because he cannot understand,he drinks
(and he drinks and he drinks and he drinks and)

not bald.   (Coughs.)   Two pale slippery small eyes

balanced upon one broken babypout
(pretty teeth wander into which and out
of)Life,dost Thou contain a marvel than
this death named Smith less strange?
                                                                Married and lies

afraid;aggressive and:American
                                                                      (*CP,* 406)

Beyond this negativity *No Thanks* at times reflects an incipient paranoia that began to overtake Cummings in his later years, an attitude
that is undeniably evident in one self-pitying item, "this mind made
war," which includes these lines:

on him they shat
they shat encore
he laughed and spat . . .
(this poet made war

whose naught and all
sun are and moon
come fair come foul
he goes alone
                                                                      (*CP,* 440)

and goes on far too long.

One might say that expressions of prickly irritation or even belea-
guered isolation are common to the satirical mood. However that may
be, Cummings' whole view of the world during the early 1930s is sometimes close to despair, as in "Jehovah buried, Satan dead," a ballade that
concludes:

King Christ,this world is all aleak;
and lifepreservers there are none:
and waves which only He may walk
Who dares to call Himself a man.
                                                                      (*CP,* 438)

As time went on Cummings' moods would continue to oscillate, ris-
ing up into elation and then dipping down into bitter depths. But high
or low, it is gratifying to find that his creativity never disappeared.

## Chapter Eight
# All These and Santa Claus Too

*No Thanks* was the product of a Guggenheim Fellowship of 1933–34, but after that burst of good fortune disappointments dogged Cummings' steps in the 1930s. Invited to California by his friend Eric Knight with the possibility of becoming a scriptwriter for a moving picture studio in Hollywood, he experienced two months of frustration in his meetings with studio executives.[1] In New York his hopes for a production of a ballet scenario based on *Uncle Tom's Cabin* came to nothing. Even though his scenario was a highly imaginative treatment, Lincoln Kirstein of the American Ballet Company, who had commissioned the work, thought it was too literary and too idiosyncratic. Nor could Cummings interest anyone else in the United States or Europe in a production despite the fact that David Diamond, a promising young composer, had completed a musical score for it. A small publishing house, Arrow Editions, finally published the scenario under the title *Tom*.

In this work Cummings drew fully on the mythic qualities in Harriet Beecher Stowe's novel. Tom is a Christ figure, Simon Legree is a satanic threat, St. Clare is the "elegant essence of Southern aristocracy,"[2] Little Eva is angelic, Topsy is "Instinct Unsubdued" (154). The climax of the work is based upon popular Christian images of the African-American Evangelical tradition, as Tom is led toward heaven by a black angel and "outward goldenly slowly the huge doors open—revealing an immeasurable radiance and which, prodigiously forthpouring upon a stage drowned in glory, becomes angels in white robes with harps of gold and crowns" (170). To this day *Tom* has never had a production, although selections from David Diamond's music have occasionally been played in concert.

## II

Cummings' career is full of surprises. In the depths of the economic depression of the 1930s he was suddenly approached by Charles Pearce of Harcourt Brace, who suggested a collected edition of his poems. Pearce selected about two-thirds of the items in all the previously published volumes and asked Cummings to add a preface and a few new poems. *Collected Poems* appeared in 1938 and became the first publication of Cummings' poems to receive a fairly widespread welcome from reviewers. The book began an upbeat period that continued through the 1940s, which turned out to be the flood tide of Cummings' creative endeavors. That decade included two collections of poetry, *50 Poems* (1940) and *1 x 1* (1944), and a play in verse, *Santa Claus, A Morality* (1946), Cummings' most successful venture in the drama.

Among the "New Poems" in *Collected Poems* three stand out: a satire on utopias that require conformity "(of Ever-Ever Land i speak)" and two sonnets, both of which involve a Romantic rejection of reason. The first begins with the lyrical wish:

> may my heart always be open to little
> birds who are the secret of living
> whatever they sing is better than to know
> and if men should not hear them men are old . . .
>
> (*CP,* 481)

The second, a love poem, rejoices in sexual fulfillment at the same time that it pushes aside intellectual activity.

> you shall above all things be glad and young.
> For if you're young,whatever life you wear
>
> it will become you;and if you are glad
> whatever's living will yourself become.
> Girlboys may nothing more than boygirls need:
> i can entirely her only love
>
> whose any mystery makes every man's
> flesh put space on;and his mind take off time
>
> that you should ever think,may god forbid
> and(in his mercy)your true lover spare:
> for that way knowledge lies,the foetal grave
> called progress,and negation's dead undoom.
>
> I'd rather learn from one bird how to sing
> than teach ten thousand stars how not to dance
>
> (*CP,* 484)

For the new poems Cummings adopted a habit of arranging his free-verse poems either into "stanzas" or into recurring patterns of lines, such as 4,1,4,1,4,1,4,1, or 1,2,3,4,4,3,2,1, or 1,3,1,4,1,3,1, so that in appearance they seem a lot less like improvisations than do some of his earlier free-verse "Impressions." He continued this practice in all of his subsequent volumes of poems.

## III

*50 Poems* begins with a mixture of linguistic and typographical excursions, satires, and light verse. One new feature in this grouping is the frequency of rhythms and patterns that are reminiscent of nursery rhymes and that occasionally include nonsense phrasing. It is heartening to see Cummings' taste for irrationality veer away from Dadaesque absurdities and turn to the tradition of nonsense, with its origins in folk literature, and which underwent a literary blossoming in the nineteenth century with the works of Edward Lear, W. S. Gilbert, and Lewis Carroll. Literary nonsense is very suitable to Cummings' temperament and philosophical outlook because, first of all, it conforms to his apprehensions about the antipoetic nature of logic, and, second, it is associated with the delight that children have in Mother Goose rhymes, jump-rope rhymes, play-party rhymes, and other primal verbal play. The appreciation for the simple, natural life of childhood had long had a place in Cummings' literary expression, going back to the "Chansons Innocentes" of *Tulips & Chimneys*. He gave it greater prominence when he specifically identified himself with childhood in *Eimi*. "I am a child," Comrade Kem-min-kz says to Madame Potiphar. "I like shining things" (64). This adoption of a child-like posture is another aspect of his role-playing: he named himself the "small eye poet" in a letter to his mother[3]; "little Estlin" or "our nonhero" in letters to friends; and "our heroless hero" in *Eimi*.

The echoes of childhood verse or nonsense rhymes occur in some of the satires. "flotsam and jetsam/ are gentlemen poeds" is directed at W. H. Auden and Stephen Spender; another satire denounces the murder and sexual violence of the Nazi and Fascist regimes:

> some like it shot
> some like it hung
> some like it in the twot
> nine months young

(*CP*, 497)

Still another, with comic bawdry, likens the persuasions of politicians to tactics in sexual bestiality. It begins this way:

> the way to hump a cow is not
> to get yourself a stool
> but draw a line around the spot
> and call it beautifool.
>
> (*CP,* 500)

The nursery rhyme form is sometimes used for a serious statement, as in "The Noster was a ship of swank," a two-stanza piece about the failure of collectivism (Noster), rationalism (Ergo), and religious authority (Pater), in the presence of individualism (Sum).

But more commonly the forms of nursery rhyme and nonsense verse are found in Cummings' celebrations of the joy in life, as in "a pretty, a day," about the ways of boys and girls together; "as freedom is a breakfast food," a tribute to love using paradoxes and twisted proverbs; "buy me an ounce and i'll give you a pound," dancing stanzas that rejoice in sex; and "love is more thicker than forget," verses that take love beyond reason in a series of nonsense comparisons.

The ultimate achievement employing the rhymes of innocence is a charming poem about "anyone" (both anonymity and uniqueness are there in the name) and his beloved "noone," and how they differ from the important personages, "someones." The passage of time is conveyed by references to sun, stars, and seasons. The structure of an idiom like "year by year" is varied to suggest the passing seasons in phrases like "tree by leaf" and "bird by snow." There is even a little nonsense refrain similar to "with a hey-nonny-no" or "heigh-ho the derry-o."

> anyone lived in a pretty how town
> (with up so floating many bells down)
> spring summer autumn winter
> he sang his didn't he danced his did.
>
> Women and men(both little and small)
> cared for anyone not at all
> they sowed their isn't they reaped their same
> sun moon stars rain
>
> children guessed(but only a few
> and down they forgot as up they grew

autumn winter spring summer)
that noone loved him more by more

when by now and tree by leaf
she laughed his joy she cried his grief
bird by snow and stir by still
anyone's any was all to her

someones married their everyones
laughed their cryings and did their dance
(sleep wake hope and then)they
said their nevers they slept their dream

stars rain sun moon
(and only the snow can begin to explain
how children are apt to forget to remember
with up so floating many bells down)

one day anyone died i guess
(and noone stooped to kiss his face)
busy folk buried them side by side
little by little and was by was

all by all and deep by deep
and more by more they dream their sleep
noone and anyone earth by april
wish by spirit and if by yes.

Women and men(both dong and ding)
summer autumn winter spring
reaped their sowing and went their came
sun moon stars rain

                                        (*CP,* 515)

   This poem contains the central myth of Cummings' life: "anyone,"
like the nonhero "i," represents the child within the man. He is power-
less and neglected by others, yet happy in whatever he does: "he sang his
didn't he danced his did." He is alienated from other people whom he
considers negative in their activities and standardized in their behavior:
"they sowed their isn't they reaped their same." As the story goes on, his
beloved "noone" joins him in his response to life no matter whether good
or bad events befall: "she laughed his joy she cried his grief." Her name
allows Cummings to express both the isolation that anyone feels and the

love that she offers: "noone loved him more by more." This same dou-
bleness (with a touch of paranoia) applies to the response to the death of
anyone: "noone stooped to kiss his face." The poem ends with the people
of the world following their fruitless routines as anyone and noone lie
buried together absorbed in the natural world, which continues its diurnal round.

The works in *50 Poems* show an increase in the number of words
uprooted from their normal grammatical places and transformed for new
metaphorical compactness. Two of them are worth a special look. One
has an arresting beginning:

> wherelings whenlings
> (daughters of ifbut offspring of hopefear
> sons of unless and children of almost)
> never shall guess the dimension of
>
> him whose
> each
> foot likes the
> here of this earth
>
> whose both
> eyes
> love
> this now of the sky . . .
>
>                                    (*CP*, 515)

By means of only two coined words ("wherelings whenlings")
Cummings creates a full statement about the existence of people in space
and time. Then with a sprinkling of surprisingly used conjunctions,
nouns, and an adverb, he compresses into two lines the information
about their parentage, the uncertainty in their sense of themselves, and
the tentativeness in their behavior.

The second is a long poem in praise of Cummings' father that is actually too long because it is a series of statements that list praises rather
than develop the poem thematically. It expresses a son's love and admiration and represents Cummings' reconciliation with a parent whom he
had regarded in earlier years as an interfering do-gooder. Its rhymed
lines begin solemnly with a metrical regularity appropriate for the
Reverend Edward Cummings,

> my father moved through dooms of love
> through sames of am through haves of give,
> singing each morning out of each night
> my father moved through depths of height
>
> this motionless forgetful where
> turned at his glance to shining here
>
> (*CP*, 520)

and continue on to transfer to his father all the features of his own views about the value of individualism and the primacy of feeling over thinking.

New developments in Cummings' personal life in the 1930s account for some of the changes in tone that are found in *50 Poems* and that are even more pronounced in *1 x 1*. Shortly after his breakup with Anne he had fallen in love with Marion Morehouse, a stunningly beautiful fashion model, who soon moved into an apartment in the court at Patchin Place, where Cummings had the third-floor studio that constituted his living quarters. Marion became the woman in his life: like "noone," "she laughed his joy she cried his grief." They were never separated thereafter, although they were never legally married. They lived together, traveled together, spent their summers at Joy Farm, shared their few possessions. When Cummings died his will bequeathed his estate to "my wife, Marion Morehouse."[4]

The change in attitude toward his father took longer. Evidence that tensions between the two began to relax first appeared in 1925, after Estlin had lived away from the parental household for six years. He sent a laudatory paragraph about his father to Paul Rosenfeld for a biographical article about his own background.[5] But after the death of Edward Cummings in 1926 the idealization of the dead parent, a common psychological occurrence, took place. It shows up in the star poems of *No Thanks* and elsewhere and most directly, after a prodding by Estlin's friend the poet Theodore Spencer, in the poem "my father moved through dooms of love." Cummings himself expressed the stages in his relationship with his father clearly and succinctly in his notes: "I loved him: first as a child, with the love which is worship; then, as a youth, with the love that gives battle; last, as a man with the love which understands."[6]

22. MARION MOREHOUSE AS SHE APPEARED IN *VOGUE*, 15 OCTOBER 1925
*Photograph by Edward Steichen, reprinted with permission of Joanna T. Steichen*

## IV

In many ways *1 x 1* represents the peak of Cummings' achievement in poetry. The volume was an advance beyond *50 Poems* in the number of carefully patterned poems, and the overall design of the collection surpassed that of *No Thanks*. There is also a central theme of "oneness" that runs through the volume, an emphasis on love that expresses itself in the idea that one times one equals one. Corresponding to its title the book divides into three parts, with the usual progression from darkness to light. Part I begins with a poem about a winter with a weak sun ("nonsun blob") and leafless trees, and it continues to another work about a modern-day Garden-of-Eden story, complete with a little apple-stealing ("it's over a (see just"). Then follow some first-rate antiwar poems. "ygUDuh," arranged in a visually distinctive pattern, is a brilliant mimicry of a New Yorker expressing his hatred of the Japanese, and "plato told" is Cummings' expression of General Sherman's assertion that "War is hell," while at the same time the poem suggests that the United States sold scrap metal to the Japanese that was later converted into the means of destruction for young Americans:

           plato told

           him:he couldn't
           believe it(jesus

           told him;he
           wouldn't believe
           it)lao

           tsze
           certainly told
           him,and general
           (yes

           mam)
           sherman;
           and even
           (believe it
           or

           not)you
           told him:i told

                   .

him;we told him
(he didn't believe it,no

sir)it took
a nipponized bit of
the old sixth

avenue
el;in the top of his head:to tell

him

                                        (*CP*, 553)

An antiwar sonnet, "(fire stop thief help murder save the world)", builds toward the idea that "the world" is really the world of nature—of mountains, pine trees, and snowfall. Among the dark entries in this section is a piece of invective railing against the mob, "Huge this collective pseudo-beast," the animal without a heart. But the depth of negation is reached in a powerful sonnet, "pity this busy monster, manunkind/ not," which ends with a curt dismissal of what human beings have done with their world:

        We doctors know
    a hopeless case if—listen:there's a hell
    of a good universe next door;let's go

                                        (*CP*, 554)

Yet Part I concludes with the first of the poems on the theme of oneness: "one's not half two. It's two are halves of one:" is a poem that decries division and even prefers dying into a new life if oneness could result: "All lose, whole find" (*CP*, 556).

Part II is a mixture of themes, halfway toward light; it includes personal poems, love poems, explorations of form—and even a poem about world catastrophe, done in the idiom of nursery rhyme:

        what if a dawn of a doom of a dream
        bites this universe in two,
        peels forever out of his grave
        and sprinkles nowhere with me and you?

                                        (*CP*, 560)

The section begins with a subtle piece about the process that takes place when a poem is being created. The poem is developed as if it were describing a snowfall. These are not snowflakes, however; they are thoughts, impulses, or words that come drifting down into consciousness. Cummings even manages to work the motif of 1 x 1 (one by wonder) into this poem.

> one(Floatingly)arrive
>
> (silent)one by(alive)
> from(into disappear
>
> and perfectly)nowhere
> vivid anonymous
> mythical guests of Is
>
> unslowly more who(and
> here who there who)descend
> -ing(mercifully)touch
> deathful earth's any which
>
> Weavingly now one by
> wonder(on twilight)they
> come until(over dull
>
> all nouns)begins a whole
> verbal adventure to
>
> illimitably Grow
>
> > (*CP*, 557)

This section of the book also contains a restrained but very effective elegy on the death of Cummings' old friend Sam Ward, the factotum who took care of odd jobs at Joy Farm. On the day of Sam's death Cummings meditated on Sam's whole approach to life and revealed how much of a model Sam had been for his own way of looking at life:

> Sam is dead—Sam Ward—I turn for comfort to Cézanne; read
> "L'art est une adaption des choses à nos besoins et à nos gouts." And
> think that's why Sam suspected me—of cowardice. For he felt I, &
> people like me, were not tackling anything, not facing something.
> We were dodging—"adapting," transforming (cleverly) a thing to
> suit our wish. And that wasn't a man's deed. . . . A man took just
> that thing ("life") as is; & wrestled it & hated it & loved it, & got
> thrown by it ("death"). Just that was all—for a man. A man isn't

clever. A man is strong, brave, tough, enduring. The clever feller
sidesteps, kids people—and himself—what's real being too much
for him, he invents & substitutes, he believes in this (or pretends to)
substitute, & pretty quick he gets a lot of other weaklings to believe
in him and in his substitute. That ain't nothing; what's real goes
right on, being handled by real men. And handling what's real is
enough for any real man: he don't have no time for anything else,
he ain't famous and rich and handsome—all that stuff don't make
no difference at all. What's real ain't handsome—it's homely; ain't
rich—it's simple; ain't famous—it's common . . . it's something
you and I didn't make and there it is, it's just something that's got
to be done; it's a chore. You got to face that chore, you got to look
that chore in the eye, or you ain't really a man. And if you ain't really a man, why you ain't really alive. But don't kid yourself—even if
you ain't never really lived you're going to really die.
      He stood like a father to me.[7]

    With thoughts like this going through his head Cummings worked
out an appropriately spare poem:

> rain or hail
> sam done
> the best he kin
> till they digged his hole
>
> :sam was a man
>
> stout as a bridge
> rugged as a bear
> slickern a weazel
> how be you
>
> (sun or snow)
>
> gone into what
> like all them kings
> you read about
> and on him sings
>
> a whippoorwill;
>
> heart was big
> as the world aint square

with room for the devil
and his angels too

yes,sir

what may be better
or what may be worse
and what may be clover
clover clover

(nobody'll know)

sam was a man
grinned his grin
done his chores
laid him down.

Sleep well

                                                (*CP,* 568)

As Nancy Wright put it, this was Cummings' version of "The Death
of the Hired Man."[8]

One of the several sonnets casts aside history, which can never capture
the life of

every madge and mabel dick and dave
—tomorrow is our permanent address
and there they'll scarcely find us (if they do)
we'll move away still further into now

                                                (*CP,* 579)

Among the many love poems one manages in three compact stanzas
to combine Cummings' enjoyment of spring, his appreciation of love, his
address to his beloved, and his rejection of reason together with his play
on grammatical elements whose semantic function has been altered for
new meaning:

yes is a pleasant country:
if's wintry
(my lovely)
let's open the year

both is the very weather
(not either)
my treasure,
when violets appear

love is a deeper season
than reason;
my sweet one
(and april's where we're)

                                        (CP, 578)

Part III is almost entirely lyric and bursting with tributes to flowers, birds, trees, love, and springtime, and includes a number of variations upon the motif of 1 x 1. It opens with an appropriately slim vision of a plant coming into bloom (a crocus?). The shortness of the lines and the splitting of the words suggests the squeezing of the shoots up through the stones. As the blossom appears, the change of a "you" to "thou" carries the sense of something intimate and precious. The poem completes its pattern by balancing a fragment of "thou" against the first word:

how

tinily
of

squir(two be
tween sto
nes)ming a gr

eenes
t you b
ecome

s whi
(mysterious
ly)te

one
t

hou

                                        (CP, 581)

23. PENCIL SKETCHES OF MARION
MOREHOUSE BY E. E. CUMMINGS.
*Courtesy of the Houghton Library, Harvard
University*

The expressions of joy in life and love culminate at the end of the book in a play-party dance-song that also, in a Wordsworthian, anti-intellectual way, thrusts aside books. Its opening stanza sets the pattern:

> if everything happens that can't be done
> (and anything's righter
> than books
> could plan)
> the stupidest teacher will almost guess
> (with a run
> skip
> around we go yes)
> there's nothing as something as one

so that Cummings can fit in lines like "now i love you and you love me/ (and books are shuter/ than books/ can be)." He rises up finally to close "with a spin/ leap/ alive we're alive/ we're wonderful one times one" (*CP,* 594). After these words, we turn the page to find that he has placed his dedication to Marion here at the end of the book.

Since this book appeared during World War II and its anxieties, Cummings said that he was "trying to cheer up my native land."[9] Readers must have been considerably cheered, for it was commercially the most successful of all his books of poems to date. It went into three printings in 1944, an English edition in 1947, and a second edition in 1954. It even pulled *50 Poems* and *Collected Poems* into increased sales.

## V

Equally cheery in spirit is a verse play, *Santa Claus: A Morality,* which, though quite short, is the first dramatic work that Cummings was able to bring to completion after wrestling off and on over the years with various schemes and ideas. It is less in the tradition of the Morality plays of the fifteenth century than that of the puppet plays that children enjoy at Christmastime, and as such, has its stereotypical figures and its simple ups and downs. The play divides into two parts, the first of which uses the Faust story of a good person tempted by evil in order to gain additional powers. The second part tells the story of Lost Loved Ones Reunited.

As the play opens, Death, strolling the streets, meets a crestfallen Santa Claus who is bemoaning the situation that he has so much to give, but can find no one willing to take of his bounty. Death, who has the

worldly wisdom appropriate to the Mephistophelian character, explains
to him what is wrong with the world:

> Imagine, if you can, a world so blurred
> that its inhabitants are one another
> —an idiotic monster of negation:
> so timid, it would rather starve itself
> eternally than run the risk of choking;
> so greedy, nothing satisfies its hunger
> but always huger quantities of nothing—
> a world so lazy that it cannot dream;
> so blind, it worships its own ugliness:
> a world so false, so trivial, so unso,
> phantoms are solid by comparison.
> But no—you can't imagine such a world.[10]

He convinces Santa Claus to become a salesman and to peddle the
easiest thing to sell, namely, "Knowledge without understanding,"
which is the product of Science. He changes masks with Santa Claus,
who is told to try to sell people something that does not exist—shares in
a "wheelmine."

In scene 2 Santa Claus is shown as a pitchman selling plenty of shares
because wheels "are things that make the world go round" (131). He
also tells "the Mob" that he is "Science." His success is cut short when a
rumor circulates that an accident has taken place in the wheelmine. As a
result, in scene 3 the Mob is pursuing Santa Claus (Science) because he
defrauded them. Death warns Santa that the only way he can escape is
to prove that he does not exist. Therefore Santa denies that he is what
the Mob thinks he is, and puts the proof up to a little girl. The Child
easily identifies him as Santa Claus. The Mob is thus thwarted because
"there ain't no Santa Claus" (135).

The second part of the play turns to the story of the Lost Loved Ones.
This time Death wants to exchange clothes as well as masks with Santa
Claus, who is seen musing about the beautiful Child. "Thinking of the
old days, eh?" asks Death. "Well, children are your specialty" (136).
After discovering that Santa Claus once loved a woman Death comments, "Well, everyone makes mistakes," and departs to see "a swell jane
up the street" (136).

According to the Romantic version of the Faust story, Woman is the
savior of Faust. In *Santa Claus* the figure is divided in two, with the Child
as savior in Part I. In Part II it is the Woman who is the savior and who

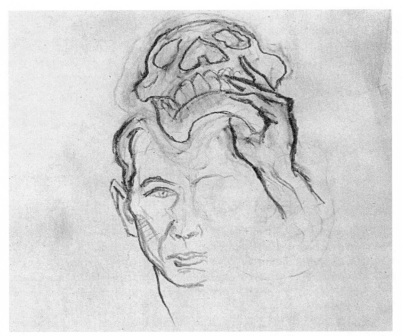

24. *SANTA CLAUS REMOVING THE MASK OF DEATH.* PENCIL SKETCH BY
E. E. CUMMINGS, 1946, INTENDED AS AN ILLUSTRATION FOR *SANTA
CLAUS* BUT NOT USED BY THE PUBLISHER.
*Courtesy of the Houghton Library, Harvard University*

now appears full of despair because she cannot find her lost love nor the
joy that was born from love. Seeing Santa Claus dressed as Death she
tells him she is ready to succumb. When Santa agrees to take her "Now
and forever" she regains hope in life, for she has heard a voice like that of
her lost love. Thus she recoils from Death and refuses his embrace. As if
she has passed a test by conquering despair, her decision sets off the next
action. The Child enters and rushes into her arms. The Woman greets
the Child as her lost "Joy." Santa Claus removes his mask to reveal the
face of a young man, whereupon the Woman "kneeling to Santa Claus"
and holding the Child proclaims "Ours" (139).

There is a deep connection between this play and Cummings' personal life. By chance he had had some recent contact with his long-lost
daughter.[11] During the war Nancy Thayer, as she was named, had

returned to the United States, worked in Washington as a translator, and married Willard Roosevelt, the grandson of President Theodore Roosevelt. From time to time friends had brought Cummings news about Nancy, but he did not attempt to make himself known to her for fear that reawakened emotions would disturb his work. When she came to New Hampshire to visit her mother-in-law in the summer of 1945 he even watched her like an unidentified Enoch Arden when she passed in the streets of Madison, near Joy Farm. He learned in September that Nancy had her first child and that he was now a grandfather. The new awareness of Nancy and her life seems to have sparked him into literary activity. In writing *Santa Claus,* with its sublimated wish for a negation of his 1924 divorce, he had his first success since 1928 in completing a play. When the play was first published in a special Cummings issue of the *Harvard Wake* in 1946 it was accompanied by his fairy tale "The Old Man Who Said Why," a story he used to tell Nancy back in the 1920s.

Once Cummings realized Nancy's reappearance was not going upset his work habits he arranged to meet her and they became friends. She had heard many years ago that her mother had once been married to

25. NANCY THAYER,
CUMMINGS' DAUGHTER.
OIL PAINTING BY
CUMMINGS, MAY 1, 1948.
*Courtesy of Nancy T. Andrews*

Cummings but she still did not know the truth of her paternity. Then one day in May 1948, when he was painting her picture in his New York studio, he revealed to her that he was her father. The news turned out to be a source of both joy and disappointment for Nancy. As time went on Cummings kept his distance from her emotionally, partly because Marion was jealous over this new bright female presence in their lives and partly because Cummings still had the notion that any emotional energy he gave her would be drained from his creative powers. The result was a confused and troubled family relationship that, sadly, had its origins in a messy sexual triangle of many years past.

# Chapter Nine
# Aches and Pains and Daffodils

The remaining years of Cummings' life were attended by health problems. As early as 1941 arthritis had begun to trouble his back and legs. Soon he was wearing a metal-braced corset that he dubbed "The Iron Maiden." Although this brought some relief his pains increased as the years went by and his journals are filled with details about his difficulties in sleeping, standing, and traveling by automobile or airplane for any extended period. In the late 1940s he began to have heart fibrillations, which caused intermittent alarm. He tried to stop smoking but usually relapsed after a short period of ill-tempered restraint. His journal entries show him full of crochets and complaints—and occasionally giving in to irrational fulminations. Cummings was beginning to feel his years.

His next collection of poems, *Xaipe* (1950), which means "rejoice" in Greek, does not have the exuberant spirit of its title. In addition to two elegies for dead friends, Paul Rosenfeld and Peter Munro Jack, the reader will find a number of poems on old age, including a tribute to the sculptor Aristide Maillol at age eighty, and other poems on death and immortality. Beyond that, one might say that the seventy-one poems offer "the mixture as before," to use Somerset Maugham's phrase. Even so, a few additional features should be singled out.

Many of the satires in the book seem overly fierce. His attack on President Franklin Roosevelt five years after the president's death seems unusually mean-spirited: "F is for foetus(a punkslapping/ mobsucking/ gravypissing poppa" (*CP*, 635). Yet we should be aware, I suppose, that Cummings' opposition to authority was so unceasing that he was hostile to all of the presidents of his adult lifetime, from Wilson to Kennedy, even though there is no evidence that he ever voted in any election.

His antiwar poems seem out of date, especially "o to be in finland/ now that Russia's here," which denounced "uncle shylock" for not coming to the rescue of Finland in World War II. That poem actually ran counter to Cummings' pronounced objection to the United States' entry into the War, a position he maintained throughout the entire four-year period. But the real folly of this publication is an epigram that brought upon him charges of anti-Semitism.

a kike is the most dangerous
machine as yet invented
by even yankee ingenu
ity(out of a jew a few
dead dollars and some twisted laws)
it comes both prigged and canted

(*CP,* 644)

This piece would have caused even more of an uproar if he had published the last line as he had originally written it, "it comes both pricked
and cunted," but he changed it when publication problems arose as early
as 1945, the year he sent it to the *Quarterly Review of Literature.*[1]
Cummings defended himself in explanations to his friends by saying that
what he meant was that a Jew who had been corrupted by American
wealth was no longer a Jew but just someone worthy of the derogatory
term "kike."

No matter what he maintained about his intentions the word "kike"
used in this blunt attack carried connotations to a civilized reader, aghast
at the recent revelations of Hitler's death camps, of hate and persecu-
tion. Quite understandably his epigram met widespread denunciation
and also became the focus of a symposium in a special issue of *Congress
Weekly* on the question of his anti-Semitism.[2] Moreover Cummings had
brought the controversy upon himself knowingly for before publication
he had been warned by two friends, the poet Lloyd Frankenberg and the
artist Evelyn Buff Segal, that this little rhyme was deeply insulting to
Jews and would cause outrage among a wide range of readers. They
urged him to withdraw it. But Cummings stubbornly refused this
advice, even indicating that he would enjoy riling the public. He was
carrying out, it seems, a frequent practice,of the paranoid personality:
doing something to enrage people so that he could complain that everyone was ganging up on him.

Actually Cummings was revealing an attitude that he had harbored
for some time. His anti-Semitism seems to have been awakened during
the summer that he spent in Los Angeles trying to land a job as a script
writer, for the journals and letters describing his experiences at that time
show a series of offensive remarks about Hollywood Jews. This prejudice
against Jews is not an isolated instance in his life. Cummings grew up at
a time and in a community of people that, however enlightened, looked
upon the recent immigrants to America in general as an inferior lot. In
the Boston area it was the Irish who had swarmed in, and young Estlin
and his friends despised the "Somerville Micks" who were their neigh-

26. SELF-PORTRAIT, OIL
PAINTING. CUMMINGS IN
THE 1950S.
*Courtesy of Nancy T. Andrews*

borhood enemies (and who put rocks in their snowballs). In later years, as New York increased its rich ethnic mix, Cummings regarded the recently arrived Italians, Irish, Poles, and East European Jews as a servant class. He felt benignly patronizing if they carried out their jobs and haughtily critical if they presumed above what he considered their station. These were, however, attitudes toward groups; he made exceptions for his friends. Indeed, always intensely loyal to friends, he would have gone to the guillotine for Jewish friends such as Paul Rosenfeld, Jere Knight, or Dr. Fritz Wittels, his psychoanalyst.

Even so, as years went by and he became increasingly touchy and irritable toward everyone his journals show frequent derogatory comments about Jews ("les choisis," as he mockingly called them) and other ethnic groups, comments that seem ironically out of keeping with the persona of his poems who frequently exhibits so much love and joy. Yet sometimes in his journals he chastises himself for these feelings and acknowledges an evil streak within that is a part of his being. "What is the

'problem of evil,' " he wrote in March 1946, "except a failure to recognize *in myself* the Hawk the Spider and the Cat—those opposites of the
Thrush, the Butterfly, and the Mouse, whom in myself, i not merely recognize but cherish with a jealous love?" He goes on to admire Thoreau's
declaration "I never met a man worse than myself."[3] Once in a while a
poem will reveal that he perceives the many selves that jostle within his
own psyche. In *Xaipe* one meditative sonnet faces up to the puzzling
complexity of his own nature:

> so many selves(so many fiends and gods
> each greedier than every)is a man
> (so easily one in another hides;
> yet man can,being all,escape from none)
>
> so huge a tumult is the simplest wish:
> so pitiless a massacre the hope
> most innocent(so deep's the mind of flesh
> and so awake what waking calls asleep)
>
> so never is most lonely man alone
> (his briefest breathing lives some planet's year,
> his longest life's a heartbeat of some sun;
> his least unmotion roams the youngest star)
>
> —how should a fool that calls him "I" presume
> to comprehend not numerable whom?

(CP, 609)

That nature included the prayerful hermit as well as the xenophobic
curmudgeon. "As I grow older, I tend toward piety,"[4] Cummings wrote
one Christmas season in 1948. Indeed Cummings grew more religious as
the pangs of mortality afflicted him. But his religiosity took various
forms. Marion was a Roman Catholic who, although she had lapsed from
ceremonial observances, still retained an awareness of the Church calen-
dar and occasionally went to church to pray. Cummings sometimes
entered her church on his daily walks to absorb the atmosphere or to
kneel in prayer before a statue of the Blessed Virgin Mary. Yet on one
occasion, while trying to compose a libretto for Paul Nordoff to set to
music, he prayed to the full moon ("I became a pagan"[5]). On another
occasion, on a visit to Tucson, Arizona, he had a mystical experience

while walking in the desert where he encountered a strange cactus-like plant: he touched one spine and jumped "spiritually 40 miles."[6] His journals are full of references to "le bon Dieu" and frequent prayers for help in his creative life (such as "Bon Dieu! may i some day do something truly great. amen."[7]). He also prayed for strength to be his essential self ("may i be i is the only prayer—not may i be great or good or beautiful or wise or strong."[8]), and for relief of spirit in times of depression ("almighty God! i thank thee for my soul; & may i never die spiritually into a mere mind through disease of loneliness"[9]). One specific entry is a more sound indicator of his true religious leanings. He had been at work on a ballade, the refrain of which was "Someone is mightier still—Christ," and he mused, "Yes, T. S. Eliot & Toynbee are right: the times call for an organized religion—no mere unitarian—'starring' a crucified savior." Then he heard a bird sing, thought of the beauty of the natural world, and wrote, "If I could . . . become one with this loveliness, truthfulsuch a truth, why then there'd be no crying on saviors to save me from my sins."[10] His basic religious feelings were more in tune with his Unitarian upbringing. His concept of God was that of a comprehensive Oneness together with a sense of the presence of this Oneness in nature. In *Xaipe* he expressed this belief most clearly in a sonnet that combined both prayer and an awareness of Divinity in the natural world:

> i thank You God for most this amazing
> day:for the leaping greenly spirits of trees
> and a blue true dream of sky;and for everything
> which is natural which is infinite which is yes
>
> (i who have died am alive again today,
> and this is the sun's birthday;this is the birth
> day of life and of love and wings:and of the gay
> great happening illimitably earth)
>
> how should tasting touching hearing seeing
> breathing any—lifted from the no
> of all nothing—human merely being
> doubt unimaginable You?
>
> (now the ears of my ears awake and
> now the eyes of my eyes are opened)

(CP, 663)

## II

Despite the aches and pains Cummings continued to be active, working at both his painting and his poetry. Indeed he developed an entirely new career giving poetry readings at colleges and universities around the country; this occupied a good part of his time and brought him sorely needed income during his last decade. In time he became the most popular American poet, aside from Robert Frost, on the poetry-reading circuit. In performance he was, with his mellifluous voice, the best reader who ever appeared before these academic audiences, save Dylan Thomas who made two spectacular American tours in the 1950s. The high point of this new adventure in public appearances was his tenure in 1952–53 as Charles Eliot Norton Professor at Harvard, where the six lectures that he delivered, mostly autobiographical reminiscences, were published as *i: six nonlectures* in 1953.

Many honors came to him in these final years. In 1950 he received the Harriet Monroe Prize of $500 from *Poetry* magazine and a fellowship of $5000 from the Academy of American Poets. In 1951 he was awarded a second Guggenheim Fellowship. In 1954 Harcourt Brace published a complete collected edition of his poetry, *Poems 1923–1954,* which was chosen for a Special Citation by the National Book Award Committee in 1955. He received the prestigious Bollingen Prize of $1000 from Yale University in 1958, and most welcome of all was a surprise in 1957 of a two-year Ford Foundation grant of $15,000.

Cummings was sixty-four years old when he published his last volume, *95 Poems,* in 1958. There is a serenity about this collection that had not emerged earlier. For one thing it is the first time one of his books reflects the full cycle of human life, for it includes a sonnet on the birth of a baby ("from spiralling ecstatically this"), inspired by the entrance into the world of Nancy's latest child. Two other poems deal with the inarticulate communication that babies have in their first months ("this little huge/-eyed pers-/on(nea" and "the(oo)is/100k").

At the other end of the life spectrum there are poems on the inevitability of death, such as "there's also dying," and one on the theme that all flesh is not grass, but flowers ("once White & Gold/daisy in the Dust"). There are many nature poems, mostly products of the increased enjoyment of life at Joy Farm, and whose subjects include a saucy jay bird, two sentinel robins, a thrush and a hummingbird, roses from "my mother's greatgrandmother's rosebush," a whippoorwill, a forest pool, the sun, moon, stars, and "the good rain the farmers pray for." The volume ends like *1 x 1* with a dance-song, "if up's the world, and a world grows greener."

There are several examples of an old technique. Cummings had many times previously trickled a poem down the page and included several fragments of accompanying phrases in parentheses. In this book he introduces a form employing parentheses in which two statements are intertwined, one of which is a subtle emanation of meaning arising from the other. As the volume opens we see a little word-construction made up of the word "loneliness" and the statement "a leaf falls," with the two elements intertwined and arranged so that the whole is broken up into nine lines:

l(a)

le
af
fa

ll

s)
one
l

iness

(*CP*, 673)

In line one the letter "l" looks just like the arabic numeral one, and the definite article "a" designates just a single leaf. Then the rest of the letters that spell out "leaf falls" are scattered down the page in five more lines as if to demonstrate how the leaf drops: the pattern of two letters to a line, at first alternating consonants and vowels, suggests a drifting to and fro. In line seven comes the word "one," which continues the spelling of the word "loneliness" but also begins to spell "oneliness"; and then "l" by itself again (it is the numeral one and it stands alone). Finally as the rest of the word "loneliness" is completed, the remaining letters acknowledge "i-ness." The effect is a compact visio-literary experience that also carries the spirit, Mitchell Morse has remarked, of a Japanese haiku.[11]

Indeed the restraint and subtlety of the Japanese aesthetic hovers over many of these poems. Another work that is made up of two intertwined and counterpointing statements is closer to a Zen koan, for the relation-

ship between the two statements is enigmatic. It sets down the words
"unmoving are you asleep," while parenthetically intruding are the
words "bee in the only rose."

un(bee)mo

vi
n(in)g
are(th
e)you(o
nly)

asl(rose)eep

(*CP*, 691)

The rose suggests the beauty of the motionless sleeper. Yet the bee
suggests motion. The beauty supine invites probing, suggested by the
bee. Other phrases in other poems of this volume carry the same mystery
of paradox that is found in Zen koans: "love is more than love" ends the
dialogue in the poem "lily has a rose"; a poem about a fortune-telling
cockatoo reaches another thought-blunting conclusion:

14th st dis(because my tears
are full of eyes)appears. Because
only the truest things always

are true because they can't be true

(*CP*, 697)

Another poem full of paradox, "in time of daffodils (who know," ends,
"and in a mystery to be/ (when time from time shall set us free)/ forget-
ting me, remember me" (*CP*, 688). The spirit of the koan as a genre
matches the tone of serene acceptance as well as the mystical tendencies
of Cummings' later years.

But no book of Cummings' work would be representative without at
least a little disruptive satire. In the doggerel rhythms that he frequently chose for his scathing attacks Cummings included a bitter Hudibrastic
poem denouncing the United States and the United Nations for their
incitement of the Hungarian Revolution and then their inaction when it
exploded and was crushed by the Soviet Union.

In a century full of disaster and injustice nothing ever enraged Cummings quite so much as the brutal totalitarian action against Hungary that the world stood by and watched in 1956. In entry after entry in his journal Cummings describes anguished conversations with friends about the situation and records meditations on the moral problem that gnawed at him: the fact that he had always been a pacifist, but now in his old age, when he would not have to fight in a war, he was angry that the United States did not go to war to protect Hungary:

> I saw war—*while I was in danger of being drafted*—as a brutally obscene collective horror . . . from which any true individual or healthy human being must immediately & entirely recoil. And O, how savagely our recoiler attacked the older generation ("my sweet old etcetera") with its eagerness for sacrificing the younger! how ferociously he satirized pro-war politicians ("after of course god america")!—he, alias I: who, today, am (as a member of "the older generation") cursing America's present government for not having risked war—or anything else—on behalf of Hungary; & hating myself for being unable to volunteer against Russia, or escape in some other way the impotence of inaction.[12]

In any case he wanted to go on record publicly about his feelings, and "THANKSGIVING (1956)" "wrote itself,"[13] combining all his detestation of Communist oppression, his contempt for the ineffectual dithering of the United Nations, his political conservatism (aimed at figures such as President Eisenhower, whom he considered a lily-livered liberal), and his usual contrariness about his own nation and its policies:

> a monstering horror swallows
> this unworld me by you
> as the god of our fathers' fathers bows
> to a which that walks like a who
>
> but the voice-with-a-smile of democracy
> announces night & day
> "all poor little peoples that want to be free
> just trust in the u s a"
>
> suddenly uprose hungary
> and she gave a terrible cry
> "no slave's unlife shall murder me
> for i will freely die"

> she cried so high thermopylae
> heard her and marathon
> and all prehuman history
> and finally The UN
>
> "be quiet little hungary
> and do as you are bid
> a good kind bear is angary
> we fear for the quo pro quid"
>
> uncle sam shrugs his pretty
> pink shoulders you know how
> and he twitches a liberal titty
> and lisps "i'm busy right now"
>
> so rah-rah-rah democracy
> let's all be as thankful as hell
> and bury the statue of liberty
> (because it begins to smell)
>
> (*CP*, 711)

When he was chosen to be the Boston Arts Festival Poet for the summer of 1957 he submitted "THANKSGIVING (1956)" as the commissioned "Festival poem," but its attack on the United States' position was so strong that the Festival committee would not accept it. Cummings promptly resigned as Festival Poet. It took an extraordinary amount of patience and delicacy on the part of the committee to bring him back in a compromise that was worked out: he would submit another "Festival poem" but "THANKSGIVING (1956)" would still be included in his poetry reading at the Festival. The new poem was a product of one of his humbler moods:

> i am a little church(no great cathedral)
> far from the splendor and squalor of hurrying cities
> —i do not worry if briefer days grow briefest,
> i am not sorry when sun and rain make april
>
> my life is the life of the reaper and the sower;
> my prayers are prayers of earth's own clumsily striving
> (finding and losing and laughing and crying)children
> whose any sadness or joy is my grief or my gladness

around me surges a miracle of unceasing
birth and glory and death and resurrection:
over my sleeping self float flaming symbols
of hope,and i wake to a perfect patience of mountains

i am a little church(far from the frantic
world with its rapture and anguish)at peace with nature
—i do not worry if longer nights grow longest;
i am not sorry when silence becomes singing

winter by spring,i lift my diminutive spire to
merciful Him Whose only now is forever:
standing erect in the deathless truth of His presence
(welcoming humbly His light and proudly His darkness)
                                        (*CP*, 749)

Both of these works took their place in *95 Poems.*

One other poem in the collection deserves comment not only because it became a favorite in his public readings but also because evidence is available about how the poem came into being. Of course, any one of Cummings' daily experiences could be a possible stimulus to his literary consciousness. These ordinary experiences would undergo his own process of absorption until they became for him symbolic scenes or actions suitable for his creative mood. One day he was taking his daily walk near Washington Square when he witnessed a pair of young people fooling around in the park:

sitting, at sunset, in the Square, notice 2 adolescents—a gotup hard-plump girl & a gangling, grinning-unhealthily youth—stand-ing in what might have been grass. First she tries & fails to pull up a "KEEP OFF" sign' then he does, but lets it stay erect. Both look guiltily around. Then, with one foot, she slowly & deliberately push-es the loosened signpost down flat on the dirt. Both then gambol clumsily away to join their pals.[14]

The scene lay in his memory and grew over time into a conflict between age and youth. Cummings, no longer young, could remember the feelings of youthful self-assertion but was now aware that the "grow-ing" he always sought was a daily growth toward aging. A poem emerged:

old age sticks
up Keep
Off
signs)&

youth yanks them
down(old
age
cries No

Tres)&(pas)
youth laughs
(sing
old age

scolds Forbid
den Stop
Must
n't Don't

&)youth goes
right on
gr
owing old

(CP, 709)

The splitting of "Trespassing" makes it possible for him to include both a French intensifier (Tres) and a French negative (pas) as well as to allow youth to "sing." The split of "Mustn't" gives old age both a positive and a negative command. The division of "growing" provides a final reminder of what youth owes to age.

*95 Poems* is clear evidence that neither physical ailments nor murky eruptions in the psyche could stifle Cummings' creativity. The summers at Joy Farm were especially good for him, and in 1962 he and Marion were planning to install some heating in the house so that they could stay every year into the late fall. Then suddenly on September 2 Estlin suffered a stroke after chopping wood. He died the next morning at the hospital in Conway, New Hampshire, a month short of this sixty-eighth birthday. He was buried in the Forest Hills Cemetery in Boston. One of the sonnets he was preparing to include in a new book of poems provides in its way his valediction:

Now i lay(with everywhere around)
me(the great dim deep sound
of rain;and of always and of nowhere)and

what a gently welcoming darkestness—

now i lay me down(in a most steep
more than music)feeling that sunlight is
(life and day are)only loaned:whereas
night is given(night and death and the rain

are given;and given is how beautifully snow)

now i lay me down to dream of(nothing
i or any somebody or you
can begin to begin to imagine)

something which nobody may keep.
now i lay me down to dream of Spring

                                                      (*CP*, 816)

## III

He is more than remembered. The poetry of E. E. Cummings has
made a lasting impact upon twentieth-century literature. For one thing
he taught his ever-increasing audience how to read him. To date four
editions of his *Complete Poems,* each with an expanded number of items,
have been published,[15] and many of his earlier volumes have been reis-
sued.[16] His poems continue to appear in anthologies, particularly those
for literary study in college courses. The persona that the poems project
has a special appeal for young, sensitive readers who are aware of the
overwhelming forces, social and political, that surround them and whose
emotions surge as they grope for ways to adjust to their world.
Cummings' self-characterization as "i," the "nonhero," expresses for
them their joy in life, their conflicts of desire, their push against authority, and their desire to grow.

For the poets who followed him Cummings' creative endeavors constituted an important example. As some have testified, he represented a
predecessor whose play with language and form had loosened up poetry.
Louis Zukofsky was simply grateful that Cummings had abolished the

138

27. CUMMINGS IN HIS STUDY AT JOY FARM, 1952.
PHOTO BY MARION MOREHOUSE.
*Courtesy of the Houghton Library, Harvard University*

convention of beginning each line of poetry with a capital letter.[17] For
Theodore Weiss, Cummings "renewed our language, tickled it wide
awake, to its surprise, in its sleepiest corners, mainly its adverbs, prepositions, articles, and adjectives. These words—mostly regarded as lowly
and anonymous menials—in the dancing democracy of his discourse
kicked up their heels and proved themselves lovely shining
Cinderellas. . . . His work encouraged me to a larger freedom and at the
same time to an appreciation for the look of a poem, its comely shape,
upon the page . . . He showed me how . . . to convert writing's normal
temporality to the spatial."[18] Robert Creeley has said that *The Enormous
Room* "probably was the work that had the most impact upon me." But
for him Cummings' influence as a poet was more subtle and pervasive:
"Cummings' authority has so permeated the conditions of poetry in this
country for the so-called modern poets of my generation that it is very
hard to say, 'Here is particularly what he did or here particularly is how I
related to him.' Yet it is just impossible for me to imagine a poetry of my

time without this poet as the context, as one of the determining factors of that context which literally led me to it or even made it possible."[19]

In addition Cummings showed the way in which he could choose ordinary scenes and experiences and make them become little myths of twentieth-century life whether they were the childhood activities of Cambridge, the street happenings of New York, or encounters with the features of rural life in New Hampshire.

As for his love poems and his treatments of natural phenomena, he was continuing the Romantic tradition in a time when the harsh realities of urbanization and the pervasive intrusions of technology were bruising the sensibilities of modern human beings and blunting the awareness of the essential self and the consciousness of individual feelings.

But the exploration of the possibilities of linguistic expression was his special contribution. His legacy to later writers was the spectacle of his pushing language to its extremes. Joyce, Eliot, Pound, Dos Passos, and Faulkner were the major innovators of his time, but Cummings did not imitate them. He responded in spirit to their work but he made his own innovations, inspired especially by the modern movements in the visual arts: Impressionism and Postimpressionism, Cubism and Futurism, Dada and Surrealism. His poetic practice shows continuing experiment and growth over a stretch of forty-five years so that like Eliot and Yeats he was a poet of two generations. Not all of his attempts were aesthetic successes, nor was he critically stringent in what he allowed himself to publish. But an extensive selection of his poetic output would yield a huge body of permanently valuable work.

Cummings' creativity was so inexhaustible that he reached into other genres as well. As in his poetry these excursions had mixed results. Yet even though *Him* was dramatically disappointing, [No Title] was only a shaggy-dog joke, and *Tom* was never given its chance to be part of the American ballet repertoire, still *The Enormous Room* and *Eimi* are lasting monuments, each of them unique.

This is not the place for an assessment of his extensive work in drawing and painting. Nevertheless we should be aware that Cummings' creative personality expressed itself continually in more than just the literary mode of art. His success in the visual arts was limited and he never became recognized as an important practitioner. But we should not forget that these extra talents gave him a perspective on language that allowed him to present his poems in new ways.

This innovative direction is the principal reason E. E. Cummings will always be remembered as one of the leading figures of the literary revolution of the early twentieth century and that his work will never disappear from the anthologies of American literature. For individual readers, moreover, his place is secure as a "Household Poet" in the way that the chief nineteenth-century poets of America were cherished. For these readers his poems will continue to amuse, awaken, instruct, inspire and, at times, to provide the deep satisfaction that attends aesthetic experience.

# Notes and References

The following abbreviations are used in the notes and text:

CP           *Complete Poems 1904–1962,* George J. Firmage, ed. (New York: Liveright, 1991).

DITM      *Dreams in the Mirror: A Biography of E. E. Cummings* by Richard S. Kennedy (New York: Liveright, 1980).

EEC        E. E. Cummings.

ER          *The Enormous Room* (New York: Liveright, 1977).

ETC        *Etcetera, The Unpublished Poems of E. E. Cummings,* George J. Firmage and Richard S. Kennedy, eds. (New York: Liveright, 1983).

HL          Houghton Library, Harvard University (Call numbers are given for items in the Cummings manuscript collection, e.g. bMS Am1892.7).

HRC, UT   Humanities Research Center, University of Texas, Cummings Papers.

SL          *Selected Letters of E. E. Cummings,* F. W. Dupee and George Stade, eds. (New York: Harcourt Brace Jovanovich, 1969).

## Chapter One

1. For a full discussion of the *Dial* and its importance in the 1920s, see Nicholas Joost, *Scofield Thayer and the* Dial (Carbondale, Ill.: 1964).

2. EEC, letter to his father, May 22, 1920, *SL,* 71.

3. *Ibid.*

4. See Ezra Pound, "a Few Don'ts by an Imagiste," and F. S. Flint, "Imagisme," *Poetry,* March 1913. Reprinted without their titles (for Flint's article is reputed to have been written by Pound) in Richard Ellmann and Charles Fiedelson, eds., *The Modern Tradition* (New York, 1965), 141–42.

5. Or was Rushworth Kidder right in asserting that Cummings intended to call attention to the comma because it had the shape of a thumb? "Cummings and Cubism," *Journal of Modern Literature,* 7 (April 1979), 285.

6. RSK, interview with M. R. Werner, 29 July 1973.

7. EEC, letter to his father, January 10, 1920, *SL,* 68.

8. bMS Am 1892.7, Miscellaneous Notes (for a poetic theory), 4a.

9. July 21, 1855. See Ralph L. Rusk, ed., *The Letters of Ralph Waldo Emerson* (New York, 1939).

## Chapter Two

1. A large amount of this material is still extant and now in the Cummings Collections at HL and HRC, UT.

2. See Appendix B, *ETC.*

3. *Ibid.,* Appendix C.

4. bMS Am 1823.4 (104), Notes for nonlectures. Cummings maintained on several occasions that Pound was his chief influence in making him aware of the visual possibilities for poetry. I mention this especially because there is a false notion abroad that in developing his visually oriented poetic style Cummings was under the influence of Guillaume Apollinaire's calligrams. Cummings stated to Charles Norman, his first biographer, that he had never seen Apollinaire's little shaped poems until long after he had developed his poetic style.

5. By 1916 Hulme's ideas were being disseminated by his London associates, Pound, Flint, Richard Aldington, Ford Maddox Ford, and even by the American Amy Lowell. See especially chapter 2, Stanley K. Coffman, *Imagism, A Chapter for the History of Modern Poetry* (Norman, Okla.: 1951).

6. *Eight Harvard Poets* (New York 1917), 9.

7. *Ibid.* 10. When Cummings republished the poem in *Tulips and Chimneys* he unfortunately omitted the title, thereby making its basic myth obscure.

## Chapter Three

1. HRC, UT, Cummings, Miscellaneous.

2. bMS Am 1892 (905), Letter, Sam Ward to EEC, December 6, 1938. Ward's letters to Edward Cummings, which were the delight of the Cummings family, do not survive. But Estlin spoke about them to his friends—and even wanted one to be published in the *Dial.* EEC revealed the source of the small "i" in an interview with Harvey Breit, "Talk with E. E. Cummings," *New York Times,* December 31, 1950, 10.

3. bMS Am 1892.7, Notes.

4. bMS Am 1823.7 (23), 142.

5. bMS Am 1823.7 (22), 73.

6. See *ETC,* "Experiments with Typography, Spacing, and Sound: 1916–17," for examples of some of the pieces he created at this time.

7. bMS Am 1892.7 (149).

8. Cummings called this his "modernist manner." I have avoided the term modernist because it seems both limiting and dated, because it has been too loosely used in literary history, and because the so-called modern movement came to an end in the middle of the twentieth century.

9. A reconstruction of this version was published in 1976, edited by George James Firmage, Liveright Publishing Corp., New York.

## Chapter Four

1. Empey, New York, 1917; Davis, New York, 1914; Seegar, *Poems,* New York, 1916; Brooke, *1914 and Other Poems* London, 1916; Oliver, London, 1915; Gibbs, New York, 1920; Reed, New York, 1919; Owen London, 1920; Sassoon, *Counter Attack* London, 1918, *War Poems* London, 1919; Dos Passos New York, 1920 and 1921.

2. See *DITM,* chapter 9 for full details.

3. All quotations from *The Enormous Room* are from the "Typescript Edition," edited by George J. Firmage (New York, 1978).

4. The *Dial,* February 1920. Reprinted in George J. Firmage, ed., *A Miscellany Revised* (New York, 1967).

## Chapter Five

1. RSK, Interview with Slater Brown, September 1971.

2. Letter to S. A. Jacobs, Spring 1924, in the Clifton Waller Barrett Library, University of Virginia.

3. *New York World,* November 8, 1923, 9.

## Chapter Six

1. For the full details of Cummings' loss of Elaine and his struggle for parental rights to spend time with Nancy, see chapters 16 and 17 of *DITM.*

2. March 5, 1959, *SL,* 261.

3. Even *The Hairy Ape* had the subtitle *A Comedy of Ancient and Modern Life in Eight Scenes.*

4. All quotations are from the first edition of *Him* (New York, 1927).

5. The ninth is enacted as a dream by Him.

6. Edmund Wilson supplied Cummings with the words for this version of the song.

7. An extensive accumulation of pages, bMS Am1823.4 (15) and bMS Am1892.7 (198), remains.

8. This was the length of the performance of the complete version of *Him* as performed by the Circle Repertory Theater (*New York Times,* April 20, 1974).

9. For an account of the rehearsals and production, see Helen Deutsch and Stella Hanau, *The Provincetown: A Story of the Theater* (New York, 1959), 170.

10. No date. Introduction by Gilbert Seldes and statements by Conrad Aiken, William Rose Benét, S. Foster Damon, Waldo Frank, Paul Rosenfeld, John Sloan, Edmund Wilson, Stark Young, and others. A copy is in bMS Am1823.8 (39).

11. *Ibid.*

## Chapter Seven

1. For full details on Cummings' visit to Russia, see *DITM,* chapter XIX.

2. *Eimi,* 8. All quotations are taken from the third and largest edition (New York: Grove Press, 1958), mistakenly referred to as the fourth edition in Cummings' preface. All subsequent citations will consist of parenthetical page numbers in the text.

3. Lili Brik was a lover of the Russian poet Vladimir Mayakovsky and the sister-in-law of the French Surrealist poet Louis Aragon. When Cummings was leaving Paris for Moscow, Aragon asked him to take some gifts to Lili.

4. Charles Norman, *E. E. Cummings, The Magic Maker* (New York, 1972), 263.

5. The first edition by Covici-Friede, 1933, consisted of a first printing of 1381 copies for which orders had been received and a second printing of a small number of copies. The second edition by William Sloane Associates, 1949, had 1500 copies, plus 1200 remaindered sets of bound sheets. The third edition by Grove Press, 1958, of over 4000 copies had the helpful preface and glossary. A new edition edited by George Firmage for Liveright is planned.

6. Other even more obscure memories intrude into the narrative: of the Azores in 1921 with Dos Passos, of his Berlitz instructor in Paris before the trip, of the news about Ralph Barton's suicide, of his telegram to Anne about her abortion.

7. For a full discussion of the genre of fictional thesaurus, see my essay "Thomas Wolfe's Fiction: The Question of Genre" in *Thomas Wolfe and the Glass of Time* (Athens, Ga.: 1971).

8. bMS Am1823.7 (22).

9. Robert McIlvaine, "Cummings' 'BrIght,'" *Explicator* 30 (September 1971), 6.

10. *New Republic,* 75 (June 7, 1933), 94–97.

## Chapter Eight

1. For full details, see chapter 24, "A Stranger in the Supercolossal West, 1935" in *DITM.*

2. *Tom,* 155, in *E. E. Cummings: Three Plays and a Ballet,* ed. George J. Firmage (New York, 1967), the most easily available edition.

3. Unpublished letter, bMS Am1823.10, August 30, 1925.

4. bMS Am1892.11 (88), October 25, 1948.

5. Paul Rosenfeld, "E. E. Cummings," in *Men Seen* (New York, 1925).

6. bMS Am1892.7 (90), Notes for nonlectures.

7. bMS Am1892.7 (219), folder 1.

8. Nancy Wright was a student in my honors seminar "E. E. Cummings and the Poetic Experiment of His Time" at Wichita State University in 1963. She is now a novelist writing under her married name, Nancy Thayer, and

author of *Stepping, Three Women at the Water's Edge,* and *Nell.*
   9. bMS Am1892.7 (225).
   10. *Santa Claus,* 138, in *E. E. Cummings: Three Plays and a Ballet.* All references are to this edition.
   11. For full details, see chapter 27, "Reunion and Revelation," in *DITM.*

## Chapter Nine

   1. In an unpublished letter to the editor, Allen Tate, on July 20, 1945, he agreed to the change but he also explained "quite incidentally: anyone who resents [poem] 3 on the ground that it's 'antiJewish' must either be méchant or eed-yoh—since my Good American point—that the kike isn't (hélas) a Jew— so heraus mit said objector." bMS Am1892.1 (142).
   2. *Congress Weekly,* 18 (20 August 1951).
   3. bMS Am1892.7 (222). Thoreau's statement, paraphrased, comes from *Walden,* chapter 1.
   4. bMS Am1892.7 (224).
   5. bMS Am1892.7 (226).
   6. bMS Am1892.7 (221), 142.
   7. bMS Am1892.7 (224), 105.
   8. bMS Am1892.7 (222), 51.
   9. bMS Am1892.7 (221), 42.
   10. bMS Am1892.7 (225), 12.
   11. RSK, Interview with Mitchell Morse, December 1977.
   12. bMS Am1892.7 (234), 234, ca. November 18, 1956. For an account of the process of writing this poem, see *DITM,* 453–55.
   13. *Ibid.* 453–55.
   14. bMS Am1892.7 (220), 64–65.
   15. *Complete Poems 1923–1962* (New York, 1972); *Poems 1905–1962* (London, 1973); *Complete Poems 1910–1962* (London, 1981); and *Complete Poems 1904–1962* (New York, 1991).
   16. *Tulips & Chimneys* (including *&*), *Is Five, Viva, No Thanks, Xaipe,* and *50 Poems;* most have been issued as "Typescript Editions" by Liveright.
   17. Quoted by Robert Creeley in his remarks at the E. E. Cummings Pre-centennial Celebration at the Jefferson Market Library, New York, October 10, 1992.
   18. From his address, October 10, 1992.
   19. *Ibid.*

# Selected Bibliography

PRIMARY WORKS

## Published Works

*Eight Harvard Poets*. New York: Laurence J. Gomme, 1917.

*The Enormous Room*. New York: Boni and Liveright, 1922. Reprinted. New York: Modern Library, 1934; New York: Liveright, 1977.

*Tulips and Chimneys*. New York: Thomas Seltzer, 1923. Reprinted as *Tulips & Chimneys*. New York: Liveright, 1976.

*&*. New York: Privately Printed, 1925. Reprinted in *Tulips & Chimneys*.

*XLI Poems*. New York: The Dial Press, 1925. Reprinted in *Tulips & Chimneys*.

*Is 5*. New York: Boni and Liveright, 1926. Reprinted. New York: Liveright, 1985.

*Him*. New York: Boni and Liveright, 1927. Reprinted in *Three Plays and a Ballet*. New York: October House, 1955.

*[No Title]*. New York: Covici-Friede, 1930.

*CIOPW*. New York: Covici-Friede, 1931.

*ViVa*. New York: Liveright, 1931. Reprinted. 1973.

*Eimi*. New York: Covici-Friede, 1933. Reprinted. New York: William Sloane, 1949; New York: Grove Press, 1958.

*No Thanks*. New York: Golden Eagle Press, 1935. Reprinted. New York: Liveright, 1978.

*Tom*. New York: Arrow Editions, 1935. Reprinted in *Three Plays and a Ballet*.

*Collected Poems*. New York: Harcourt Brace, 1938.

*50 Poems*. New York: Duell, Sloane and Pearce, 1940. Reprinted. New York: Grosset & Dunlap, 1960.

*1 x 1*. New York: Henry Holt, 1944. Reprinted. New York: Harcourt Brace, 1954.

*Santa Claus*. New York: Henry Holt, 1946. Reprinted in *Three Plays and A Ballet*.

*Xaipe*. New York: Oxford University Press, 1950. Reprinted. New York: Liveright, 1973.

*i: six nonlectures*. Cambridge: Harvard University Press, 1953. Reprinted. New York: Atheneum, 1963.

*Poems 1923–1954*. New York: Harcourt Brace, 1954.

*95 Poems*. New York: Harcourt Brace Jovanovich, 1958.

*73 Poems*. New York: Harcourt Brace Jovanovich, 1963.

*Selected Letters of E. E. Cummings.* F. W. Dupee and George Stade, eds. New York: Harcourt Brace Jovanovich, 1969.
*Complete Poems 1923–1964.* New York: Harcourt Brace Jovanovich, 1972.
*Etcetera: The Unpublished Poems of E. E. Cummings.* New York: Liveright, 1983.
*Complete Poems 1904–1962.* New York: Liveright, 1991.

#### Unpublished Materials

Letters, journals, notes, manuscripts. E. E. Cummings Collection, Houghton Library, Harvard University.
Manuscripts (chiefly poems from early years). E. E. Cummings Papers, Humanities Research Center, University of Texas.
Letters, manuscripts of *The Enormous Room, Eimi,* and *No Thanks.* Alderman Library, University of Virginia.
Letters and manuscripts. The *Dial* Collection, Beineke Library, Yale University.

SECONDARY WORKS

#### Bibliographies

Firmage, George J. *E. E. Cummings: A Bibliography.* Middletown, Conn.: Wesleyan University Press, 1960. A descriptive bibliography of primary works.
Rotella, Guy L. *E. E. Cummings, A Reference Guide.* Boston: G. K. Hall, 1979. An annotated bibliography of secondary sources.

#### Biographies

Kennedy, Richard S. *Dreams in the Mirror: A Biography of E. E. Cummings.* New York: Liveright, 1980. A fully researched biography, drawing upon the Cummings manuscripts at Harvard, Texas, Virginia, and elsewhere and upon interviews with Cummings' friends and relatives.
Norman, Charles. *The Magic Maker: E. E. Cummings.* New York: Macmillan, 1958. Reprinted as *E. E. Cummings: The Magic Maker.* New York: Duell, Sloan and Pearce, 1964. Revised and expanded, New York: Bobbs-Merrill, 1972. A journalistic rather than critical work that deals with EEC's public rather than private life.

#### Criticism—Books

Baum, S. V. *E. E. Cummings and the Critics.* Lansing: Michigan State University Press, 1962. A provocative collection of critical essays from 1922 to 1954.
Cohen, Milton. *Poet and Painter, The Aesthetics of E. E. Cumming's Early Work.* Detroit: Wayne State University Press, 1987. An excellent study based on research in the Cummings papers at Harvard and Texas. Fully illustrated in color and black and white.

Fairley, Irene. *E. E. Cummings and Ungrammar*. Searington, N.Y.: Watermill Publishers, 1975. A linguist's study of the poetry, guided by the theories of Jacobson and Chomsky.

Friedman, Norman. *E. E. Cummings: The Art of His Poetry*. Baltimore: Johns Hopkins University Press, 1960. The best critical study.

_____. *E. E. Cummings: A Collection of Critical Essays*, 1972. A standard selection of essays.

_____. *E. E. Cummings: The Growth of a Writer*. Carbondale: Southern Illinois University Press, 1964. Follows EEC's career and treats all his literary work.

Joost, Nicholas. *Scofield Thayer and the* Dial. Carbondale: Southern Illinois University Press, 1964. A history of the *Dial* with illustrations from EEC's line drawings.

*Journal of Modern Literature* 7 (April 1979). Special Cummings Issue. Poems, documents, and critical essays.

*Language and Literature* 9 (1984). Special Issue on E. E. Cummings. Essays critical and linguistic.

Kidder, Rushworth. *E. E. Cummings, An Introduction to the Poetry*. New York: Columbia University Press, 1979. A book by book commentary on Cummings' work with close attention to many poems.

Marks, Barry. *E. E. Cummings*. Boston: Twayne Publishers, 1964. A critical study of limited aims: analyses of "a relatively small number of poems."

*Spring, A Journal of the E. E. Cummings Society*. A continuing publication since 1980. Information about EEC and commentary on his work.

Triem, Eve. *E. E. Cummings*. Minneapolis: University of Minnesota Press, 1969. A sensitive but brief introduction to EEC and his work.

*Wake* 5 (Spring 1976). Cummings Issue. Memoirs, appreciations, and critical assessments.

Wickes, George. *Americans in Paris 1903–1939*. New York: De Capo Press, 1980. One chapter contains a good account of Cummings in France.

## Criticism—Articles

Baum, S. V. "E. E. Cummings: The Technique of Immediacy," *South Atlantic Quarterly* 53 (January 1954), 70–88. EEC's use of space and his attempts to catch the effect of "all-at-oneness."

Bishop, John Peale. "*The Poems* and Prose of E. E. Cummings," *Southern Review* 4 (Summer 1938), 173–86. Commentary on EEC's style that reaches its fullest development in *Eimi*.

Blackmur, R. P. "Notes on E. E. Cummings' Language," *Hound & Horn* 4 (January–March 1931), 163–92. A major critical attack on EEC for his having "lost sight of meaning altogether" in his stretching of syntax and grammar and lack of precision in diction.

_____. "Twelve Poets," *Southern Review* 7 (Summer 1941), 201–5. A review of *50 Poems*, expressing admiration for EEC in his "development of fresh conventions in the use of prepositions, pronouns, and auxiliary verbs in the guise of substantives," although still holding reservations about his vocabulary and rhythms.

Cowley, Malcolm. "Cummings: One Man Alone," in *A Second Flowering, The Works and Days of the Lost Generation* (New York: Viking, 1973), 90–113. An account of EEC's career as New England individualist.

Fairley, Irene. "Syntactic Deviation and Cohesion," *Language & Style* 6 (1973), 216–29. EEC's irregular syntax is used for patterning and organization.

Fraser, G. S. "The Aesthete and the Sensationalist," *Partisan Review* 22 (Spring 1955), 265–72. EEC as a representative American poet of the twentieth-century.

Friedman, Norman. "E. E. Cummings and His Critics," *Criticism* 6 (1964), 114–33. Traces the critical reception of EEC's work decade by decade.

Gaull, Marilyn. "Language and Identity: A Study of E. E. Cummings' 'The Enormous Room," *American Quarterly* 19 (Winter 1967), 645–62. Commentary on the effect of EEC's unusual handling of language to convey his unusual experience.

Honig, Edwin. "Proud of His Scientific Attitude," *Kenyon Review* 17 (Summer 1955), 484–91. EEC as the most distinctively American poet among the moderns.

Kidder, Rushworth. "Cummings and Cubism: The Influence of the Visual Arts on Cummings' Early Poetry," *Journal of Modern Literature* 7 (April 1979), 255–91. The best treatment of the relationship between the poetry and the painting, with many illustrations.

_____. "E. E. Cummings' Painter," *Harvard Library Bulletin* 23 (April 1975), 117–38. Critical study of EEC's whole career as a painter, with black and white illustrations.

_____. "Twin Obsessions: The Poetry and Painting of E. E. Cummings," *Georgia Review* 32 (Summer 1978), 342–68. The relations between EEC's work in these two arts, with several illustrations.

McIlvaine, Robert M. "Cummings' 'brIght'," *Explicator* 30 (1971) 6. Analysis of the linguistic pattern of the poem.

Olsen, Taimi. "Language and Silence in *The Enormous Room*," *Spring* 1, New Series (October 1992), 77–86. EEC's handling of space in his prose, plus his appreciation of "aural space" in the silent or inarticulate characters.

Pearce, Roy Harvey. "The Poet as Person," *Yale Review* 41 (March 1952), 421–40. Emphasis on EEC's lyricism.

Rosenfeld, Paul. "The Enormous Cummings," *Contempo* 3 (25 July 1933), 1–3. A perceptive commentary on *Eimi*, recognizing the spirit of both Mark Twain and the Transcendentalists in the book.

Spencer, Theodore. "E. E. Cummings," *The New Republic* 110 (3 April 1944), 475–76. EEC and the poetry of joy and awakening.
Von Abele, Rudolph. "Only to Grow: Change in the Poetry of E. E. Cummings," *PMLA* 70 (December 1955), 913–33. Discusses both technique and theme in demonstrating the growth of the poet.
Waggoner, Hyatt. "The Transcendental and the Extraordinary: E. E. Cummings" in *American Poets from the Puritans to the Present* (Boston: Houghton Mifflin, 1968), 511–25. Recognizes EEC's use of tradition while at the same time going beyond it as a modern poet.

# Index

# The Author

Richard S. Kennedy, Professor Emeritus at Temple University, has also taught at the University of Rochester, Wichita State University, and the University of Nijmegen in the Netherlands as a Fulbright Fellow. He was educated at UCLA (B.A., 1942), University of Chicago (M.A., 1947), and Harvard (Ph.D., 1953). He served as a lieutenant in the U.S. Navy, 1942–1946. He is the author of *The Window of Memory: The Literary Career of Thomas Wolfe* (1962), *Dreams in the Mirror: A Biography of E. E. Cummings* (1980), and *Robert Browning's* Asolando: *The Indian Summer of a Poet* (1993). He has edited *The Notebooks of Thomas Wolfe* (1970), *Etcetera: The Unpublished Poems of E. E. Cummings* (1983), *Welcome to Our City* by Thomas Wolfe (1983), *Beyond Love and Loyalty: The Letters of Thomas Wolfe and Elizabeth Nowell* (1983), *Thomas Wolfe: A Harvard Perspective* (1983), *The Starwick Episodes* by Thomas Wolfe (1989), and *Literary New Orleans* (1992). He has served as president of the Society for the Study of Southern Literature, the Thomas Wolfe Society, and the New York Browning Society.

# The Editor

Joseph M. Flora earned his B.A. (1956), M.A. (1957), and Ph.D. (1962) in English at the University of Michigan. In 1962 he joined the faculty of the University of North Carolina, where he is now professor of English. His study *Hemingway's Nick Adams* (1984) won the Mayflower Award. He is also author of *Vardis Fisher* (1962), *William Ernest Henley* (1970), *Frederick Manfred* (1974), and *Ernest Hemingway: A Study of the Short Fiction* (1989). He is editor of *The English Short Story* (1985) and coeditor of *Southern Writers: A Biographical Dictionary* (1970), *Fifty Southern Writers before 1900* (1987), and *Fifty Southern Writers after 1900* (1987). He serves on the editorial boards of *Studies in Short Fiction* and *Southern Literary Journal*.

## Twayne's United States Authors

These recently published Twayne titles are available by mail. To order directly, return the coupon below to: Twayne Publishers, Att: LP, 866 Third Avenue, New York, N.Y. 10022, or call toll-free 1-800-323-7445 (9:00 A.M. to 9:00 P.M. EST).

| Line # | Quantity | ISBN | Author/Title | Price |
|--------|----------|------|--------------|-------|
| 1 | _____ | 0805740007 | WARD / *Rita Mae Brown* | $22.95 |
| 2 | _____ | 080573967X | MERRILL / *Norman Mailer* | $23.95 |
| 3 | _____ | 0805776400 | HILL / *Lee Smith* | $22.95 |
| 4 | _____ | 0805740074 | SCHIFFER / *Richard Stern* | $21.95 |
| 5 | _____ | 0805776389 | BAKER / *Studs Terkel* | $22.95 |
| 6 | _____ | 0805739858 | EVANS / *Anne Tyler* | $21.95 |
| 7 | _____ | 0805776427 | WINCHELL / *Alice Walker* | $20.95 |

Sub-total _____

Please add postage and handling costs—$2.00 for the first book and
75¢ for each additional book _____

Sales tax—if applicable _____

TOTAL _____

|  | Lines | Units |
|---|---|---|

Control No. [_____]    Ord. Type [SPCA]    [_____]

___ Enclosed is my check/money order payable to Macmillan Publishing Company.

___ Bill my ☐ AMEX  ☐ MasterCard  ☐ Visa  ☐ Discover    Exp. date _____

Card # _____ Signature _____

*Charge orders valid only with signature*

Ship to: _____

_____

_____ Zip Code

**For charge orders only:**

Bill to: _____

_____

_____ Zip Code

For information regarding bulk purchases, please write to Managing Editor at the above address. Publisher's prices are subject to change without notice. Allow 4–6 weeks for delivery.          Promo # 78700  FC2542